Great Athletes
from our First Nations

Vincent Schilling

Second Story Press

Library and Archives Canada Cataloguing in Publication

Schilling, Vincent, 1967-

Great athletes from our First Nations / by Vincent Schilling.

(The First Nations series for young readers) Includes bibliographical references.

ISBN 978-0-9779183-0-0

1. Indian athletes—Canada—Biography—Juvenile literature. 2. Indian athletes—United States—Biography—Juvenile literature. I. Title. II. Series: III. First Nations series for young readers

GV697.A1S35 2007   j796.092'271   C2007-900936-0

Printed in Canada on recycled paper

Second Story Press gratefully acknowledges the support of the Ontario Arts Council and the Canada Council for the Arts for our publishing program. We acknowledge the financial support of the Government of Canada through the Book Publishing Industry Development Program.

Canada Council   Conseil des Arts
for the Arts   du Canada

Published by
Second Story Press
20 Maud Street, Suite 401
Toronto, ON
M5V 2M5
www.secondstorypress.ca

— *Dedication* —

I would like to dedicate this book to two people: my father, Ray Schilling, who taught me kindness, compassion, and honesty, and to my beautiful wife, Delores, without whom I could not have accomplished this much.

— TABLE OF CONTENTS —

Acknowledgements

This book has been a fantastic journey for me, as well as a great gift. I spoke with amazing athletes who were full of enthusiasm and humility. Their accomplishments have been impressive. I feel honored to have transcribed their life's efforts. (I hope I have done all of you justice.)

I would like to thank Warren Jefferson, Jerry Hutchens, Gwynelle Dismukes, and Bob Holzapfel, who led me through the publishing process with kind words, constructive criticism and friendly advice. Thank you so much. I would also like to thank Henry Martin for his moral support and use of his resources. Thank you to those who have shown their loving support: Mary Schilling, Sharon Anderson, Mary and Parker Keller. And once again, thanks to a group of incredibly talented athletes whose lives will help shape and improve the lives and aspirations of a new generation of athletes.

Introduction

These stories you are about to read illustrate how to make a dream come true, and still stay connected to the family and heritage that are part of your inner strength. In every case, these dreams were nurtured by family, friends, or coaches, or a combination of supporters. Delby Powless credits his coach, Paul Wehrum, with putting him on the right track at a time when he was distracted by partying. Beau Kemp followed in his father's footsteps and got his motivation from his desire to please his dad. The majority of people in this book had tremendous support from their families, whether they were adopted or with their natural parents.

Each of these stories begins with a dream, a vision, a desire. And each athlete set goals and proceeded to achieve them one by one, step by step. Despite obstacles, setbacks, and resistance, these men and women kept going in the direction of their heart's desire. Each of them chose NOT to be a victim—of circumstance or discrimination—but a victor in the game of life. Sports was the avenue that allowed them to succeed in that choice, but these same inner qualities can be applied to any path a person decides to follow.

For all, a major source of their inner strength has been their Native heritage. This connection was powerfully demonstrated by Alwyn Morris when he bowed his head and raised an eagle feather on the Olympic platform as a symbol of his Native roots and the spiritual messenger that had visited him during his training.

Often, there were many difficulties to be overcome, proving success is the embodiment of talent and perseverance. *Cory Witherill* showed incredible perseverance in the face of multiple serious injuries to win his spot in the Indy 500 championship race. *Mike Edwards* came back from a devastating loss that might have ended another bowler's career, risking his reputation to push beyond his failure and achieve a crowning victory. And then there is *Cheri Becerra-Madsen*, who triumphed over a triple set of obstacles. As she explains it, "I'm not only a Native, I'm also a woman, and in a wheelchair." Cherie became an Olympic and Paralympic medal winner, and world record-holder in her field.

All of these athletes have used their success to be a force for good in their own communities. Almost everyone here has an organization, program, or affiliation that promotes opportunities for Native youth, or has opened the door for Native people in a sport where there were no people of color at all. In giving back, these athletes have made their success complete, for they are nurturing a new generation with the potential to achieve even more.

Sports itself offers many benefits. The physical activity involved can help thwart issues of obesity, diabetes, and other health-related problems that currently face Native and non-Native youth alike. The guidance, direction, and self-discipline provided by sports can help raise self-esteem, and steady progress toward a chosen goal can be an ongoing source of empowerment. Time spent in athletics means less time spent in bored isolation or destructive behaviors, and local sports events create opportunities for social interaction and bonding among families and neighbors.

People of all colors and genders, ages and occupations can be motivated and guided by these stories. I hope they will open you up to new possibilities for your life, or give you added motivation to continue on your chosen path. Whatever the case, I encourage you to dream an amazing dream for yourself and then go out and live it.

Great Athletes
from our First Nations

Richard Dionne

CBA Basketball Champion

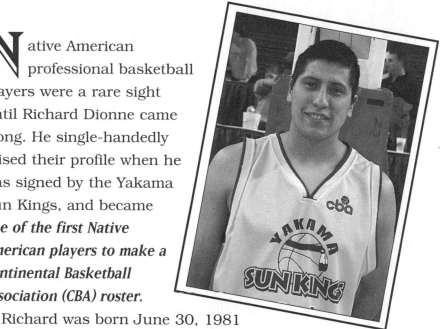

Native American professional basketball players were a rare sight until Richard Dionne came along. He single-handedly raised their profile when he was signed by the Yakama Sun Kings, and became *one of the first Native American players to make a Continental Basketball Association (CBA) roster.*

Richard was born June 30, 1981 in Williston, North Dakota, and he was raised in Poplar, Montana on the Fort Peck Reservation. Richard was the oldest child in the family and a fine big brother to his three younger sisters. His parents created a close and stable environment; but beyond the immediate family circle, there was a lot of pain and sadness.

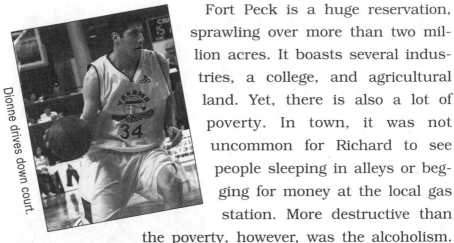

Dionne drives down court.

Fort Peck is a huge reservation, sprawling over more than two million acres. It boasts several industries, a college, and agricultural land. Yet, there is also a lot of poverty. In town, it was not uncommon for Richard to see people sleeping in alleys or begging for money at the local gas station. More destructive than the poverty, however, was the alcoholism. Three of Richard's uncles drank themselves to death, and Richard remembers the devastating effect on their loved ones. "It really put our family through tremendous heartache." That pain would lead to one of the most important decisions of his life: to concentrate only on positive things.

By the summer before seventh grade, Richard was taller than average and a natural athlete. It was no surprise, then, that he began playing basketball. He also participated in football and track in junior high. By eighth grade he was six feet (1.8 m) tall, and the following summer before he entered high school, Richard grew another three inches (7.6 cm). "That is when my knees really started to bother me. I found out I had Osgood Schlatter disease. I was really sore during my high school freshman year. I have this extra lump and it looks like I have another kneecap on my knee."

Osgood Schlatter occurs most commonly in children aged ten to fourteen who are highly active and experiencing a strong growth spurt. Kids feel a tightness of their thigh muscles combined with pain and swelling just below the kneecap. Usually Osgood Schlatter goes away after a few months. It did in Richard's case, and he could then focus on high school sports, pain free.

Richard attended Poplar High School, running cross-country all four years and helping his team become state champions three years in a row. In his junior and senior years, Richard was All-State in cross-country (top fifteen), track (top six), and basketball. Richard and his team won the district basketball championship and came close to winning state.

Despite his success in sports, growing up was not easy in his small community. Peer pressure was enormous and alcohol was everywhere. But Richard had seen the misery alcohol could bring, and he made a pledge to his mother:

> **"I promised my mom that she would not have to worry about me doing that kind of stuff, even though a majority of my friends were hanging out with the juniors and seniors who were partying. But, knowing what I knew about addiction, I just wasn't into it. Plus, I was also deathly afraid of my mom. She's got a look on her! If looks could kill—just being looked at was, like, wow! "**

Richard has kept that promise. *To this day, he has never had a sip of alcohol or taken any type of drug.*

15

After high school, Richard went to Miles Community College. In his freshman year, he led the Pioneers basketball team in scoring, averaging 16 points per game, and played a huge part in his team's conference win. During his sophomore year, he raised his average to 22 points per game.

After his second year at Miles, Richard was approached by scouts from several four-year colleges. He was initially interested in Texas Pan-America, but decided to check out a couple of other schools. "I went to see the University of Nebraska at Kearney and absolutely loved my visit down there. The guys treated me well, the coaches were awesome, and it was a winning program. In Texas, they were rebuilding the team, and I didn't want to be a part of a team that was rebuilding." Richard decided on Nebraska-Kearney almost immediately. "It was probably one of the best decisions I had ever made."

Nevertheless, Richard says, he began to feel homesick. "My junior year was a little rough for me. I wasn't playing very well. It was the first time I was a long way from home. I missed my family and I wanted to come home.

> **"I had a long conversation with my mom one night. She told me, 'You made a commitment to be with this team. They are paying for your school and you owe it to them to be there and to do what you can.' She told me pretty much, don't be a quitter."**

Richard didn't quit, although he had only a nine-point per game average that year. His senior year, however, was a different story. Nebraska-Kearney made it to the NCAA Division II Elite Eight. Richard had helped his team win 32 of 35 games, and averaged 11.8 points, 3.7 rebounds and 1.2 assists per game.

After his graduation from university, he went back to Miles Community College and helped coach the Pioneers, the team he had played for just three years previously. "I was an assistant coach for one year. It was a great experience, but it wasn't for me quite yet." He longed for something more—and that something was just around the corner.

At that time, a man named Nelson Hernandez was organizing an exhibition game for the Native American Youth and Elder's Foundation (NAYEF) basketball team. Nelson had heard about Richard's talent and invited him to play for the Native team against the Yakama Sun Kings. "In the exhibition game," Richard recalls, "we played against the Sun Kings—and we got spanked. I scored 34 points, but we ended up getting beaten by something like 30 points."

Despite the one-sided score, it was obvious that Richard had outstanding skills. So it was no surprise when the Yakama Kings offered Richard a contract.

Richard looks for a shot.

"They got my number after the game. They said they were thinking about bringing me in because I was a good shooter. I was like, 'All right, I'll take a look at the contract.' I had been working at a boys and girls ranch as a counselor back in Montana, and I was making okay money. But when they said, 'We will pay you this amount every week,' I said, 'Well shoot, it looks good to me.' I signed the contract on Wednesday, November 16, 2005. They flew me home that day. I got my car, got a bunch of clothes, and ended up driving back to Yakama. It was a fifteen-hour drive. I got there late Thursday night, and we had a game the next day."

That Friday night, Richard Dionne played his first game as a professional, in the Continental Basketball Association. As he had just arrived, he was unfamiliar with any of the team's plays and strategies, so he was on the court only a few minutes. "I scored two points and had a couple of rebounds, and I got about five or six minutes of action. But that was the

— Basketball —

Basketball is very popular in the United States, and unlike most sports, has no ancient history behind it. The game was literally created overnight by James Naismith, who was at one time the athletic director of McGill University in Montreal. Naismith created the game for a Massachusetts YMCA.

Listening to the coach is important to an athlete's
performance and the team's success.

beginning. Ever since then, I have been living the dream
I've had ever since I started playing basketball—to play as
a professional. Scoring those two points was pretty neat."

Richard's dream is far from over. At the end of the sea-
son, he and his fellow Yakama Sun Kings won the CBA
Championship against the Gary, Indiana team, the Steel
Heads. In his first year as a professional basketball player,
*Richard Dionne won the honor—for both himself and all Native
people—of wearing a championship ring.*

Richard intends to speak at basketball camps, warning
children of the dangers of drugs and alcohol. He hopes that
relating his personal knowledge of the deadly effects of alcoholism will make a lasting impression on his listeners.

He also has other experiences to share with his young audiences.

> **"I would just tell kids coming from a small town, like I came from, 'It's okay to have big dreams—because with hard work, determination, and sacrifice, anything is possible.' One of the main things that I tell kids at home is that the most important thing is hard work—hard work and discipline."**

ABOUT FORT PECK RESERVATION

Fort Peck Reservation is home to Fort Peck Community College. This two-year public school is chartered by the government of the Fort Peck Assiniboine and Sioux Tribes. Located in Poplar, Montana, Fort Peck Community College offers nine associate of arts, six associate of science, and ten associate of applied science degrees.

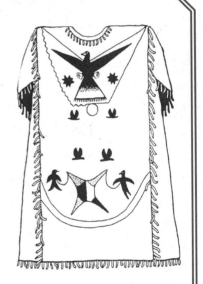

Cheri Becerra-Madsen

Olympic Bronze Medalist,
Paralympics gold, silver and bronze medalist, and World Record holder

When you hear of someone with a "disability" you may think of a person whose ability to perform everyday tasks is limited. But for Cheri Becerra-Madsen, a Native American of the Omaha tribe who has been paraplegic since the age of four, the sky's the only limit she respects.

Cheri is a spectacular success: a *two-time Olympian, Paralympian, and World Record holder in three-wheeled wheelchair racing.* She has earned respect for women, her Native heritage, and people with disabilities worldwide.

Cheri Becerra was born in Nebraska City, Nebraska. When she was four years old, a virus left her paralyzed from the waist down. "All my brothers and sisters would be out riding their bikes," she remembers. "I'd go riding, too, but I couldn't keep up in my wheelchair. They were too fast." The solution?

> *Cheri rode on the backs of their bikes.*
> *Sometimes they would tease Cheri in a good-*
> *natured way, because she was always losing her*
> *shoes. According to Cheri, "That is so funny,*
> *because I still lose my shoes."*

When Cheri was eighteen, a teacher friend read a magazine article about three-wheeled wheelchair racing, and asked Cheri if she would be interested in going to a meet being held a couple of weeks later. "That was the first time I had even seen a racing chair. When I got there, there were all these kids in these chairs, and they were really fast. I tried to compete with them in my everyday, regular chair, and they smoked me!"

At the event, Cheri met Jim Martinson, an amputee and Vietnam War veteran. Jim is the designer of the Shadow three-wheeled racing chair. He let Cheri use his chair in the competition, even though it wasn't a very good fit. "He was a grown man, and I was a really skinny girl. I've always been less than a hundred pounds. He was rolling up shirts and stuffing them into the chair so I wouldn't move around so much. Also, it was different than my regular chair, because you race leaning over. My chest was on my lap, and I remember my back hurting, because I don't think I had ever been in that position." But in spite of Cheri's back pain, she found success. "I ended up beating almost everyone there—my first time ever in the chair!"

After that first race day, she considered taking up racing, but did not have the $3,000 for a new three-wheeled wheelchair. Cheri was in for a big surprise. Her home town threw a benefit that raised enough money to buy one. After that, there was no stopping her.

Soon Cheri was invited to the nationals. With only two weeks to train for them, she had to learn a whole new way of moving in a wheelchair. "I would wear what are called harness gloves. You kind of punch the rim, so the gloves have to be able to stick to the wheel. You never grab it, only punch off on it. Your hands are always in a fist. When I went to the nationals, it was a real awakening, because everybody there was fast. I thought it was going to be pretty easy. I didn't realize the competition that was out there."

Even against the best racers in the country, Cheri came in first in her age category. In fact, she finished in the top three over all, losing by only by a half-chair length! Jim Martinson was delighted, and offered to sponsor her on the spot. "He custom-fitted me with a new wheelchair. It was specialized, with tri-spoked wheels, and all that jazz."

At that meet, Cheri made friends with wheelchair racer Leanne Shannon. They hit it off instantly, and when Leanne asked if Cheri would like to come to Florida to train, Cheri accepted.

Leanne lived in Jacksonville, Florida, and though Cheri was happy to have a new friend, she was unaccustomed to such a quiet a house. "There are six of us kids in my own family. My house was always loud. Total screaming, total chaos, everybody arguing—Leanne's was different, but it was nice."

Cheri and Leanne would go to the gym early in the morning. Sometimes during the day they would get on a hand cycle, an elongated three-wheeler, peddled by hand. At night, they would go to the track. Cheri and Leanne both had their sights set on the national trials, the qualifiers for the Olympic and Paralympics Games.

The Olympics offer two events for wheelchair athletes: the 1500-meter race for men and the 800-meter race for women. The Paralympics take place just after the Olympics, at the Olympic sites. There are Paralympics competitions for paraplegics, quadriplegics, amputees, and the blind, among others. Through hard work and determination, Cheri eventually won enough events to qualify for the Paralympics. And after that: the 1996 Olympics.

"Our regional meet would be in the US. Then we would do our semifinal in Europe. So you have a chance of getting beat out twice before you get to the Olympics." If she did well enough in the US trials, she would get to go to the semifinals.

Well enough? She won the US trials! On to Paris!

Cheri attended the Fédération Française de Handisport, the training center for athletes with disabilities in France, under the guidance of US coach and wheelchair athlete Marty Morris. There, Cheri had a whole new experience: discrimination.

❝I'm not only a Native, I'm also a woman, and in a wheelchair. I got all these things thrown at me that I didn't even know existed until I got out there and tried to rule the world, no longer pampered by my family.❞

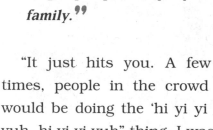

"It just hits you. A few times, people in the crowd would be doing the 'hi yi yi yuh, hi yi yi yuh" thing. I was called a Yankee. I was, like, 'Dude. Do you know what a Yankee is? I'm a Native American. I'm so not Yankee.' But I always got the war cry thing. It was dumb, but they thought it was funny." Even so, Cheri proved she was ready to handle anything. At a competition just before the Olympic trials, *she broke the world record in the 400-meter!*

At the Olympic trials, Cheri came in with a strong finish and found herself on the US Olympic team, along with Jean Driscoll, and her friend, Leanne Shannon.

At 10 a.m. on August 1, 1996, Cheri was at the starting line for the 800-meter race at the Olympic Games in Atlanta, Georgia. After an intensely competitive race, she took the bronze medal with the time of 1:55.49, and became *the first Native American female to win a medal in the Olympic Games.*

Cheri proudly displays her racing equipment, Olympic jacket, and medals.

In the Paralympics, a couple of weeks after the Olympic closing ceremony, *Cheri won bronze medals in the 400-meter and the 800-meter races, and took the silver in the 100-meter and the 200-meter races.*

At first glance, Cheri Becerra had a lot to overcome, being a Native American, a woman, and a paraplegic. But nothing was going to keep her back. Right after the 1996 Paralympics Games, she began training for the Paralympics and Olympic Games that would take place in Sydney, Australia in 2000. There, she had a huge disappointment: she came fifth in the women's 800-meter Olympic race.

Rather than getting depressed or angry with herself, Cheri transformed her dissatisfaction into determination. In the Sydney Paralympics, she not only won the gold medal in both the 100-meter and the 400-meter races, *she broke two world records!*

— *Paralympics* —

The Paralympics were created for athletes with physical (amputee, paralyzed or other impairment) and sensorial (such as blindness) disabilities. Competitive wheelchair racing is one of many Paralympic events and involves the use of a specialized 3-wheel racing wheelchair. The Paralympics hold multiple races for wheelchair racing. Athletes can win a bronze, silver or gold medal in the 100, 200, 400 and 800 meter events.

After she retired from competition, Cheri moved to Union City, a small town near Nebraska City—just a post office and a few hundred people who mostly know one another. She is married, has two daughters, and lives next-door to her mother. She believes strongly in pursuing your dreams and speaks out against drug and alcohol abuse, and other things that shatter those dreams time after time.

> **"If you have a dream, you've got to focus on it and do it. It's really important to be involved in sports or some extracurricular activity that is going to be a positive influence. I can't wait for my girls to grow up and be involved in sports. It's going to be so cool."**

ABOUT THE OMAHA

Over 6,000 Omaha continue to live near their ancestors' original settlements along the Missouri river in eastern Nebraska and a small portion of Iowa. Their traditional base, now part of the Omaha Tribal Reservation and adjacent counties, totals 2,594 square miles. A treaty with the United States signed on March 16, 1854 establishes the Omaha Tribe's legal hold on reservation lands.

Cory Witherill

Professional Race Car Driver

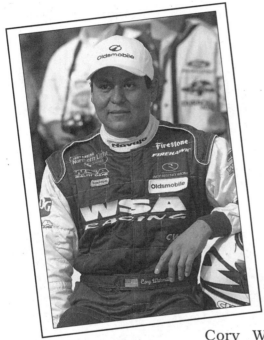

Few people will ever know the thrill of hurtling around a racetrack at 230 miles (370 km) per hour. Cory Witherill does. In 2001, he became *the first Native American driver to race in the Indianapolis 500.*

Cory Witherill's mother was from the Navajo Nation, near the Four Corners Region where Arizona, Utah, Colorado, and New Mexico meet. She was only eighteen when she became pregnant, and felt that she could barely take care of herself, let alone an infant. Wanting the best for her baby, she put him up for adoption.

Cory became the youngest of Liston and Carol Witherill's ten official children. The Witherills had an amazing way with kids and their unofficial family was much larger than ten.

Youngsters who had no place to go, or who had a difficult family life, were always welcomed and given support and guidance. The Witherills stressed self-esteem and hard work. Cory remembers one boy in particular. "My brother met him down at the beach. My mom fed him and gave him a place to live on one condition: 'Turn your life around and be something.' He did, and today he's a fireman—my dad got him into the Fire Academy."

The family spent summer vacations at Lake Arrowhead, California, and it was there that Cory got his first taste of speed. Every year, his family rented all-terrain vehicles (ATVs), and by the age of twelve he was racing around on his own. When a family friend decided to sell a Suzuki 185, it became Cory's Christmas present. By the end of Christmas

Cory's success depends a lot on working closely with his pit crew.

Day, he and his brothers had carved out a mini racetrack in the front yard.

Cory was fourteen when he competed in his first ATV race, at Ascot Park in Gardena, California. Despite being very nervous, he came in third. Cory went into his second race hungry for first place. "I caught up to the guy who was running second, and I passed him. I was getting a good momentum when I landed off a jump on a weird angle." He zoomed off the track and crashed into a parked van.

Despite torn ligaments and a broken ankle, Cory plunged back into racing. His parents agreed to support him, provided he stay away from drugs, stay in school, and get good grades. If his grades fell, he couldn't race.

While in high school, Cory broke his wrist in a race, but that didn't stop him. He was still wearing the splint in one of his last amateur ATV races. "I think I was in fourth place. The sun was going down and the track was really dusty. The four of us were bumper to bumper. I caught the glare of the sun and dust. The guy in front of me slammed on his brakes and we collided. Next thing you know we're both flying over our handlebars. His ATV landed on my arm and fractured the two forearm bones."

The result? Two plates and fourteen surgical screws remain in his arm.

Cory's doctors told him to quit racing. If he fell the wrong way, the metal could shatter his arm bones beyond repair. Cory still wanted the speed and the adrenaline rush of competing, but compromised. He'd race dune buggies—they came with seat belts!

Over the next few years his wins included five Valvoline de Montréal Off Road Championships and two PACE US Stadium Off Road Championships. *To this day he is "the man to beat" in off-road racing.*

In 2000, Cory passed the Indy Racing League rookie test. That made him eligible to compete in the Indy Lights, a series of races that allow drivers to develop their skills in Formula 2000 cars, which are lighter, slower (about 140 miles (225 km) an hour) versions of IndyCars.

At 130 mph (209 kph), as Cory tells it, "The Formula 2000 cars are safe, but they're mainly for road-course racing. They have an all-metal tubular frame, not designed to take a hard impact. But going into turn three, I got hit, and compressed and fractured my T6 vertebra. I had to have a back brace on for about eight weeks." Cory was taken off the course in an ambulance, but back racing a mere twelve weeks later.

As the cars he drove got faster, racing became more physical, so Cory decided to step up his physical training. He made a bet with a friend that he'd stick to it—and he did, jogging every morning and going to the gym. Within three months, Cory went from 183 to 167 pounds, greatly improved his fitness level, and found it easier to control his vehicle.

In 2001, Cory was asked to race for a team that had competitors in the Indianapolis 500. To qualify, he had to have one of the 33 fastest runs. Sounds easy? Maybe not—the time between first and last place is less than one second.

Cory had three days to get his speed over 220 mph (354 kph), but for the first two days he could not do it. He had never driven at such speeds.

"When I was coming out of turn four I could see an airplane in the corner of my eye. A plane lands at 200 miles (322 km) an hour and I was passing the airplane when it was coming down for a landing. That was my eye opener. But I was only going 219 (352), and running out of time."

Cory's team decided to change the degree of placement of his tires by a mere four millimeters; but after four practice laps he asked them to adjust it halfway back—two millimeters. He had one hour left in which to qualify! All of his training and years of dedication came down his speed in these last four laps.

— Indy Auto Racing —

The Indianapolis 500 is the fastest long distance car race of its kind in the world. Held annually on Memorial Day, this race is known for racecars that travel at an average of 200 miles per hour. A racecar driver must possess the ability to drive for extended periods of time. They must also exhibit endurance, quick reflexes and intuition in order to handle such a high-powered racecar. Although all of these skills are important, proper care and maintenance of the vehicle by a pit crew can be the difference between winning and losing a race.

He was one of the last drivers to secure a spot, at 221 mph (355.6 kph). "I qualified on the final hour of bump day, the third day," and was **the first full-blooded Native American to qualify for the Indy 500.**

There were four hundred thousand people at Indianapolis Motor Speedway during the Memorial Day weekend in late May, 2001. Cory recalls that bleachers towered about as high and long as in a football stadium on both sides, pretty much all the way down the front straightaway to the first turn. "It was wall-to-wall people!" The drivers arrived at six in the morning and still needed police escorts to ease them through the throngs of race fans.

Cory started in thirty-first place, but soon made his way up to twelfth, competing against drivers he had admired for years—Al Unser Jr., Johnny Rutherford, Michael Andretti, Jimmy Vasser, and Rick Mears. In lap 140, he caught up to Arie Luyendyk, two-time winner of the Indy 500. "I had him locked in my sights, and I was gaining on him and I would've probably been able to pass him."

Suddenly, Cory's car spun out of control. He'd run over some debris and punctured a tire, which sent his car heading for the wall. "I just closed my eyes and braced myself and waited for the impact. Two cars were coming straight at me. It looked like they were going to T-bone me. But then they locked up the brakes and turned away. Meanwhile, I was sliding sideways down the front straightaway. I missed the wall by about a foot."

Cory's car was towed back to pit; the team worked feverishly, and got him back in the race. By now he was down ten laps and in twenty-sixth place, but he worked his way up to nineteenth before the time ran out.

> **"When I came back from Indy, my brother gave me a big hug. I showed him a picture taken a half hour before the race—they have all the drivers line up at the start/finish line. Then it all sunk in! This was something I had wanted to do when I was a kid, something I spent my whole life working on. I was like, Wow—did I just do that?"**

With hard work and dedication, Cory lived one dream, but he has many more. He hopes to become the first Native American to win both the Indy 500 and the Daytona 500. He also dreams of becoming the first Native American to race full-time for a NASCAR team.

Cory's biggest dream, however, is to stop the rise of diabetes among Native Americans. In 2003, he created a program called Team Diabetes Racing (TDR) to encourage Native Americans to take control of their health. He travels around the country making presentations to raise awareness about diabetes and the importance of exercise and proper diet.

Cory also encourages young people to stay away from smoking, drugs, and alcohol, and to follow their dreams. He has even established an internship program to help Native American kids interested in racing achieve their goals. As he tells the young people he talks with:

"You really have to want to do it. Otherwise, you're just wasting your time. Like anything in life, if you do it, you have to do it right."

ABOUT THE NAVAJO

The Navajo Nation covers 25,000 square miles, situated within the exterior boundaries of Arizona, New Mexico and Utah. There are approximately 225,000 members of the Navajo Nation, making it largest federally recognized Indian tribe in the United States. Several thousand non-members also reside and work on the Navajo Nation.

Alwyn Morris

Olympic Kayaker

Standing on the Olympic podium to receive a gold medal is probably the peak of any athlete's career. *When kayaker Alwyn Morris stood there at the 1984 summer Olympics medal ceremonies, he proudly held aloft an eagle feather* to honor those who had helped him achieve his dream— his family, his

Mohawk ancestors, and Canada. Alwyn and his partner, Hugh Fisher, won both bronze and gold medals for their efforts that year.

Alwyn Morris was born in 1957, in the Mohawk territory of Kahnawake, south of Montréal, Québec. The Kahnawake kids didn't have any league sports, but they played hockey in the winter, and lacrosse and a little bit of baseball in the summer. Alwyn also spent his free time with friends swimming in the nearby lake.

Alwyn grew up in a very disciplined atmosphere. Both his strict Catholic family and highly regimented Catholic school handed out harsh penalties for misbehavior. Alwyn had to go to confession daily and to Mass three or four times a week. If he wanted spending money, he had to earn it, which he did by caddying at the local golf course.

Alwyn was always especially close to his grandfather, Tom Morris. Tom became very sick while Alwyn was still quite young and he moved in with his grandparents to help his grandmother. After Tom recovered, Alwyn stayed on at their place and learned valuable lessons from them.

Alwyn and his grandfather, Tom Morris, in 1958.

❝When you have grandparents around you, you learn to appreciate the quality of the individual, because they're coming from a point of wisdom and experience that is far deeper than anyone else's.❞

Alwyn's grandfather had been a successful athlete, prominent in both lacrosse and hockey, and was a wonderful role model for his young grandson.

In 1968, while watching the Mexico City summer Olympics on TV, Alwyn announced that he was going to be in the Olympics someday. When Tom asked his grandson if he realized how much work that would involve, twelve-year-old Alwyn told him that no amount of work was too much. He was determined to be an Olympian, even though he hadn't chosen a sport.

Fate stepped in when the Onake Paddling Club opened up in Kahnawake the year Alwyn turned fifteen. He joined, and before long was on the first rung of the ladder to his Olympic dream. But Alwyn was small and thin. His coaches didn't think he would ever amount to any kind of real athlete. Was he going to let that stop him? "Is being small a hurdle? If you let that take control of you, it will be! There are a lot of things that make up an athlete. It's not just about size, it's not just about strength. It's a combination of many different pieces that give you the fortitude and other characteristics to compete at the highest level."

No matter what people said—bystanders, teammates, or even coaches—Alwyn was going to prove them wrong, with discipline, drive, and positive thinking. Soon, his hard work began to pay off. His club coach, Kenneth Deer, noticed that instead of just hanging out with friends or getting into trouble, Alwyn was always on the water, practicing. In time, he became the club's number-one paddler. He progressed steadily and started to win some competitions.

The motivation behind all this practice and dedication was advice he had received from his grandfather.

"If you intend to get anywhere," Tom Morris had told him, "you not only have to work hard, but you also have to ask yourself a couple of questions. First, did you give all that you possibly could? If you answer yes, then you have to be satisfied, and move on. If you answer no, you have to ask, why didn't I? Second, did I get as much out of this day as I possibly could have or did I cheat myself?"

In 1975, two special things happened: Alwyn won the Canadian national junior championships, and tryouts for the 1976 Olympics were held in Montréal. Because of his national win, Alwyn and his doubles partner, Jean Fournel, were invited to compete for a place on the Canadian Olympic team. The pair made it to the finals, although they did not place.

Alwyn said, "I missed it by a bit, but trying to make the Olympic team in 1976 had its major benefits the following year, because I was able to get to a much higher level of training."

It was the possibility of advanced training that forced Alwyn to make one of the biggest decisions of his life. The best training in Canada was in Burnaby, British Columbia, almost three thousand miles west. Three thousand miles from parents, friends, and most important, from his grandfather. Although it would be lonely being separated from the people who were important to him, Alwyn decided to go to Burnaby.

There, the young paddler met and became friends with Hugh Fisher, who would eventually become his Olympic partner. He also received a gift that was both an inspiration and a wonder: "A Great Bald eagle would come to the training site every spring and every fall, and sit on these big, big trees or perch on top of the poles that marked out our kayaking course."

The eagle has the keenest sight of all birds and flies the highest. It is said to be the earth creature closest to the world of the Spirit, and a messenger who carries people's hopes and prayers to the Creator.

Alwyn and Hugh's faces show the determination and perseverance that are required to succeed in sports or any endeavor.

"So I started to speak to him in my Mohawk language—it just seemed to be the right thing to do. And when I spoke Mohawk, the eagle seemed to become interested and perked up. He moved his head, as if he understood, as I drifted in my kayak next to his post.

"I continued to speak to him and all the other guys were, like, 'Look, he's listening to you!' It was so cool. This majestic bird just stood there and listened to the words I was saying, and allowed us to approach so close. It was only after I paddled away that he took off. Knowing the range of these birds and that each one controls certain areas, my assumption is that it was the same bird that came every year."

Alwyn had his sights set on the 1980 Moscow Olympics, but he knew he would be up against superb competition. He knew that he would have to be prepared both mentally and physically in order to do well.

— *Kayaking* —

A kayak is similar to a canoe except the pilot is enclosed within the kayak itself while the canoe is open to the elements. The paddle of a kayak has a blade at both ends and the operator can paddle with both arms alternately with a smooth fluid motion. Kayaking is one of the oldest forms of transportation in the world, having been developed by the Aleuts of the Arctic regions of America and Greenland.

❝I feel there are two main approaches to facing a competitor. The first approach is to go after your competitor as if you're saying, 'I hate you so much I want to beat you.' The other approach is to say, 'I respect how good you are and that respect will help me to beat you.' I saw my competitors as athletes who had skill, who had potential, who trained really hard. That has to be recognized and respected. Not everybody goes for that. Some people go for the throat; but it has never worked for me.❞

Alwyn made the Canadian Olympic team in singles, but all the country's Olympic athletes then were dealt a devastating blow. Canada joined sixty-four other nations in an Olympic boycott. They would not send teams to compete in the Games in Moscow because the USSR had invaded Afghanistan. This was a terrible let down for Alwyn. "I was ranked in the top three kayakers in

Alwyn holds up the eagle feather as he and Hugh Fisher accept the Olympic medal.

the world for the 1000-meter singles race. It was a huge disappointment."

It was all the more disappointing because at about this time Alwyn's grandfather died. Tom Morris would never see his grandson in Olympic competition.

"I could've got stuck there—given up on it all—but the goal was still there. That's when Hugh Fisher and I partnered up, and from there, we just took it forward." Forward all the way to the 1984 Olympics in Los Angeles, California.

Alwyn and Hugh were favorites in the 500-meter and 1000-meter kayak doubles. After a bad start in the 500-meter race, they pressed hard enough to win the bronze. They were disappointed, but tried to shake it off, laughing and joking to help them refocus.

In the 1000-meter race, the German team got off to a really great start; Alwyn and Hugh were trailing. Alwyn knew that the Germans planned to go hard all the way, but there was no way they would be able to keep up their initial pace. The Canadian team had a chance! As the Germans tired, Alwyn and Hugh took the lead and never gave it back.

It was a moving moment when Alwyn stood on the podium to receive his gold medal, holding up that eagle feather. *It was widely publicized and brought attention to the culture of indigenous peoples.* Alwyn—the Canadian-Mohawk Olympic hero, the skinny kid who would never become an athlete—came home to a hero's welcome, cheered on by thousands of proud well-wishers.

His Olympic gold medal brought new opportunities and honors. The National Native Role Model Program sent him into the Native communities to encourage the youth to develop their potential and pursue their dreams.

> **❝I always hope that somewhere someone is going to get the message I got growing up, a transference of wisdom and hope, so that someone else will have the kind of an opportunity I had.❞**

In time, Alwyn became the National Spokesman for PRIDE Canada (the Parents Resource Institute on Drug Education), supporting programs to prevent drug and alcohol abuse and helped set up other organizations to help young Native people, including the Aboriginal

Alwyn Morris, outstanding athlete, the day he was inducted into the Sports Hall of Fame.

Sports Circle and The Alwyn Morris Educational and Athletic Foundation. He twice won the Tom Longboat Award for Canada's outstanding Aboriginal athlete, was appointed Ambassador of Youth for Canada, and named to the Order of Canada. *In 2000, Alwyn and Hugh Fisher were inducted into the Canadian Sports Hall of Fame.*

Today Alwyn Morris, father of twins, serves his people as Associate Director of the Mohawk Council of Chiefs, and for the Mohawk Council of Kahnawake, which negotiates with the Federal government on territorial, financial and legal matters. As always, Alwyn's goals are clear and he works tirelessly to reach them.

ABOUT THE MOHAWK

Mohawks, the "People of the Flint" are one tribe of the Six Nations, also known as the Iroquois Confederacy. They call themselves the Haudenosaunee (ho dee noe sho nee), meaning "People Building a Long House." The Haudenosaunee are the oldest living participatory democracy on earth. The United States representative democracy drew much of its original inspiration from the Haudenosaunee.

Naomi Lang

Ice Dancer and US Olympian

Skating enthusiasts know the name Naomi Lang well. After all, this ice-dance champion has been impressing audiences since she was six years old. By the time she was twenty-three, Naomi had become the *first Native American female athlete to participate in the Olympic Winter Games*.

Naomi, age 8, at a powwow in Grand Rapids, Michigan.

Naomi was born December 18, 1978 in Arcata, California, but moved to Michigan when she was eight. She is a member of the Karuk tribe by her father's heritage; her Karuk name is **Maheetahan**, which means "Morning Star."

Almost from the moment she could walk, Naomi wanted to dance. By the time she was three, she had already started ballet training. Her first performance was at the ripe old age of six, as a bonbon in Tchaikovsky's ballet, The Nutcracker. (This Christmas performance is a great opportunity for ballet students, as there are many roles for children of all ages.) After that, Naomi danced in The Nutcracker every single year until she was fifteen. At one audition, she was chosen over almost two hundred other girls.

When she was twelve, Naomi was accepted into the ballet program at the prestigious Interlochen Arts Academy in Michigan. At the end of that school year, she had done so well that the Academy presented her with an Outstanding Achievement in Ballet award, and invited her back on scholarship.

But dance wasn't Naomi's only passion. When she was eight, she was taken to a performance of the Smurfs on Ice, and left the arena completely awestruck. Soon after, she began skating lessons, and *won her first skating competition— the Springtime Invitational in Ann Arbor, Michigan—when she was only nine.*

A year later, not long before an important skating competition, Naomi caught pneumonia, which makes you very tired and feverish. It settles in your lungs, and makes it hard to breathe deeply. Did Naomi bow out of the competition? Far from it. As weak as she felt, she gave it her all and won a bronze medal.

Now Naomi was at a crossroads. She could stick with ballet and accept the scholarship to the Interlochen Arts Academy, but she was also a talented skater. How could she give up one for the other? She couldn't, and she didn't. Instead, she combined both her loves and became an ice dancer.

It was a tough decision. Had she stayed with ballet, her expenses would have been covered; but there were no scholarships or funding for a young ice dancer at her level. Naomi's mother, Leslie, was a single parent and skating is a very expensive sport. Ice time has to be rented. Then there is the cost of travel to and from competitions and living expenses while competing. Costumes have to be custom-made, stage make-up and hair have to be perfect, and even beginners' skates cost almost a hundred dollars a pair.

But the most important thing—and the most expensive— is the right coach and choreographer. Private coaches are very picky about which skaters they will work with. Fortunately, Leslie and Naomi met Sue and Eve Chalom at a skating competition in Detroit and they all quickly became good friends. Sue's daughter Eve was being trained by the famous coach, Igor Shpilband. Sue was so impressed with Naomi's talent and grace on the ice that she recommended Naomi to Igor and, after watching her skate, he agreed to coach her. But there was a catch: Naomi  needed better skates than the ones she was wearing, and high-quality ice-dance skates cost $900 a pair! No chance. But Sue and Eve Chalom came to the rescue. Eve bought new skates, and gave her old ones to Naomi.

There was only one more problem to solve. As Leslie put it, "Your average home town does not usually have an Olympic-level skating coach." And Allegan, Michigan, where she and Naomi were living, was no exception. Since Igor was based in Detroit, Leslie and Naomi moved there. Now Naomi could be coached full-time by Igor at the Detroit Skating Club.

Naomi was a natural, graceful and elegant, and was soon partnered with John Lee. In 1995, Naomi and John were awarded the U.S. Novice Ice Dance title, and in 1996 were silver medalists in the U.S. Junior Ice Dance Championships.

Talented Russian-born ice dancer Peter Tchernyshev saw Naomi skate at the 1996 Nationals and was impressed. When he discovered that her partnership with John Lee had ended shortly after that competition, he wrote Naomi a letter asking if she would be interested in meeting with him. Perhaps they would make good ice-dancing partners. Naomi traveled to Lake Placid, New York, where he was based, danced with Peter, and realized they were well-matched.

Naomi and Peter have perfected many difficult and graceful moves.

This discovery forced Naomi to make another tough decision. If she was to become Peter's partner she would have to move to Lake Placid to train with his coach, Natalia Dubova. She would have to leave behind her school, her friends, and her coach. And she was too young to go alone—her mother would have to move, too. Together they decided it was worth the hardships. Lake Placid would be their new home.

Lake Placid was a lot different from Detroit, and Naomi knew no one there except Peter. Going to a new high school, where she was a complete stranger, was hard enough, but, in Lake Placid, figure skating wasn't all-important, as it had been at the club in Detroit. Hockey was the primary sport— so hockey teams got all the prime ice time. Naomi had to train whenever the ice was free, sometimes as late as three a.m.—and she still had to be on time for school the next morning! Even so, Naomi stayed on the honor roll her entire year at Lake Placid High School, and received the Principal's Award for Excellence In Citizenship.

Naomi and Peter trained hard and made their competitive debut as a senior dance team during the 1996/1997 season. They came in fifth at the U.S. Nationals in 1997, an amazing accomplishment for skaters who had been together for so short a time.

Despite their success, Naomi was still lonely. She missed her friends and Igor, her former coach. After almost a year in

— Ice Dancing —

Ice dancing combines the formal and technical aspects of figure skating competition with the beauty and artistry of dancing. Partners of ice dancing incorporate different styles of dance and ice skating technique into their programs. You may see such dances as the tango or the Lindy combined with difficult technical moves. For the person who likes both figure skating and the art of dance, this sport is for you!

Lake Placid, Naomi returned to Detroit. Peter soon followed, and the pair began training with Igor Shpilband and Liz Coates.

All that training and hard work paid off. In 1998, the couple came third at the 1998 U.S. National Championships. In 1999, in Morzine, France, Naomi and Peter were tenth at the Challenge Lysiane Lauret World Championships, their first international competition. *For five years, from 1999 to 2003, Naomi and Peter came first in Ice Dancing at the United States Figure Skating Championships*, and they ranked as high as eighth at the world-championship level. At the Four Continent Championships, they placed third in 1999 and 2003, second in 2001, and first in 2000 and 2002.

All championship-level athletics take a toll on the body, and Naomi and Peter were forced to withdraw from the first half of the 2001/2002 competitive season after Peter suffered a stress injury. But they were determined to make a comeback, because they had one more dream—competing in the 2002 Olympic Winter Games. After Peter recovered, they went back to work on the ice. On February 18, 2002 in Salt Lake City, Naomi and Peter finished in 11th place

Naomi passes the torch at the 2002 Olympic Winter Games in Salt Lake City.

and *received a standing ovation from the Olympic audience*. As they took their bows, hundreds of yellow roses rained down on the ice from the fans.

Naomi Lang had competed in the Olympic Winter Games—something no Native American woman had done before. At a reception after the finals, Utah Indian tribes honored Naomi. Tribal leaders expressed their admiration and appreciation, and presented Naomi with gifts. Naomi had brought great honor to her tribe, her family, and herself.

In 2003, after Naomi and Peter won their fifth consecutive first place U.S. Figure Skating Championship title in Ice Dancing, they temporally retired from skating. Naomi coaches and now lives in New Jersey. On August 26, 2004, Naomi gave birth to a daughter, Lillia Ashlee Besedin. Lillia's Karuk name is *Kuusrah Imkata'xrih*, which means "Bright Moon."

On September 17, 2005, Naomi and Peter came out of retirement to perform a new program at an event to raise funds for ice-dancing scholarships. At that time, they embarked on a new career as professional ice skaters.

Looking back, Naomi's proud mother, Leslie, says that she was overwhelmed at the Opening Ceremonies of the 2002 Olympics, when she saw Naomi walk out as a part of the U.S. Olympic Team. The standing ovation that Naomi and Peter received after their free dance at the Olympics will always stand out in her mind. But there are many other accomplishments that make her proud. Looking back at her daughter's success, Leslie says:

"I think of the little moments when Naomi showed good sportsmanship, congratulating and applauding a competitor who had done well. Or the many times when her coaches, fans, and friends told me what a nice person she was."

When Naomi was very young, Leslie gave her a poster for her bedroom. It is of a beautiful ballet dancer, and it says,

'To be somebody special—believe that you are.'

Naomi Lang is someone special. She had the determination not to give up, and to prove that through persistence, passion, and hard work, anything is possible.

Many young skating hopefuls look up to Naomi and she is often greeted by fans who want her autograph.

ABOUT THE KARUK

The Karuk persist with astounding vigor in northwestern California. The traditional center of the Karuk world is where the Salmon and Klamath rivers come together. Karuk are important players in managing wildlife and protecting sacred sites.

Beau Kemp

Professional Baseball Pitcher

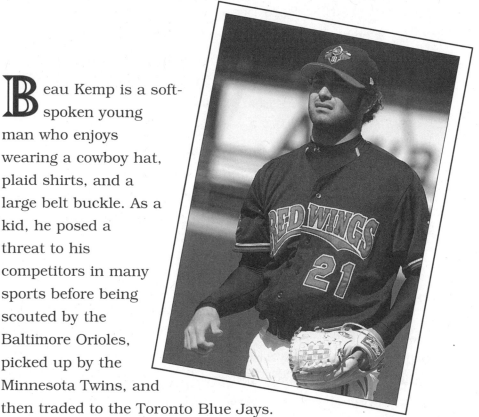

Beau Kemp is a soft-spoken young man who enjoys wearing a cowboy hat, plaid shirts, and a large belt buckle. As a kid, he posed a threat to his competitors in many sports before being scouted by the Baltimore Orioles, picked up by the Minnesota Twins, and then traded to the Toronto Blue Jays.

Sebastian "Beau" Kemp was born on October 31, 1980, in Claremore, Oklahoma. His mother was a teacher at Beau's high school. His Choctaw and Chickasaw father energized his ability in sports. "My Dad went to a boarding school, and

he never really had anything except for sports. He was a basketball player, and still plays basketball today."

Like many kids from families with no money to spare,
seven-year-old Beau spent his free time at the local Boys
Club. There were a lot of Native American and African-
American children both there and at his school. Everyone
mixed in pretty well, so Beau did not personally experience
much racism. By the age of eight, while Beau was pitcher
and shortstop with the Boys Club team in Broken Arrow,
Oklahoma, he was picked up by the Tulsa Union Rangers,
a sponsored team. As Beau explains,

> **"A sponsored team is way more competitive
> and travels both in and outside the state to
> various towns and tournaments. And the
> sponsors pretty much pay for everything: brand
> new uniforms, even new gloves—and this is for
> kids eight and nine years old!"**

The Tulsa Union Rangers went to the Little League World
Series in Atlanta, Georgia, and came fourth against tough
competition and powerful teams. "We had some rain, and
helicopters would come and dry off the field—that was a big
deal. I don't think I ever saw anything like it before
or since. And seeing teams from all over—teams
like Puerto Rico and California—that was also a
big deal."

When Beau was eleven, the Tulsa Union
Rangers won the Dizzy Dean World Series in

Chattanooga, Tennessee. "It was unbelievable. We won it pretty confidently. I pitched in that championship game."

Beau had proved himself a worthy player and played on a sponsored team every season until he was fourteen. Little League teams traveled a lot, so Beau got to see many places he would otherwise never have been able to visit.

Beau was the only freshman on a team of seniors. He was the number-two pitcher on his team, second only to Brad Penny, who currently plays for the Los Angeles Dodgers. "I pitched all four years, and in my sophomore year, we won state. I ended up getting all-state player of the year in 1997."

For most of his young life, he had been an intense competitor in football and basketball as well as baseball. In fact, Beau had been so impressive, he received competing college offers to play different sports.

He wanted to make the right choice. He also wanted to be successful, and make his father proud.

> **"I always wanted to please my Dad. He was really driving for me to be a basketball player. He knew me, and he knew what I was capable of doing, whether I was letting up or not. Sometimes he would push me and I'd get upset, but that was exactly what I needed."**

"I signed a football scholarship to North Eastern Oklahoma to play quarterback. I was going to go there for two years and then I was going to go to Oklahoma State. I was verbally committed to them to go there for football after I finished my schooling at NEO."

Beau's decision about his future got easier after he and his Amateur Athletic Union high school baseball team, the Kansas City Monarchs won the AAU National Championship, and **Beau was awarded Most Valuable Player of the tournament.** "That was the biggest moment of my life. I was pitching, and I got two or three hits. When the score was tied, I hit a little dribbler down third, and just ran as hard as I could. I couldn't see what was going on, but I was like, man, I'm going to beat this out, and if we beat it out we're defi-

nitely going to go up a run. And I ended up beating it out.

"I'm pitching and that's all I needed—to get up one run. I pretty much knew I had my A-game. So I was right there. And we won the game."

That series was the deciding factor: Beau's future would be in baseball. Meanwhile, the Big League scouts were watching. "Out of high school, I was drafted by the Baltimore Orioles, but

Beau pitching for the Red Wings.

I just held out. I don't know why, but I did. It was just a gut feeling."

It could have been his only chance to sign with a major league baseball team, but Beau had faith in himself: he was determined to be a success on his own merit and his own terms. "I talked to Baltimore, but just didn't want to sign with them. And they were like, 'Okay. We're just going to put you back into the draft.'"

After high school Beau decided to go to to Saddleback Junior College in Orange County, California. "I played for the Saddleback team, in the Orange Empire Conference. It's a real competitive league. There were scouts there when we played ball, and the Twins ended up getting me in the thirty-first round. So I was like, okay, yeah, this is what I want to

— Baseball —

Known as the "All-American Sport," baseball's name arises from the four "bases" that form a diamond shape around the pitcher's mound. In baseball, a batter attempts to hit a pitched ball that is thrown over home plate. Points are scored if a baseball is hit without being caught and the batter runs a complete revolution around the bases.

Baseball's influence is far-reaching: in literature it is popularized in the poem "Casey at Bat," written by Ernest L. Thayer, and in music, the familiar song "Take me out to the ball game," is sung by crowds at baseball games today.

do. I'm going to go into professional ball. I know that's exactly what I want to do now and I'm going to do it."

Now that's self-confidence.

Once accepted by a professional baseball team, players climb the ranks of minor-league clubs. Beau climbed very quickly. "There are two rookie-ball leagues. Then there's A-ball. Then there's Double A. And then there's Triple A, and then the big leagues. My first year, I went to rookie ball, and I was there for almost a month, before going to higher rookie ball. That team was the Elizabethtown Twins. We won our league, so I ended up winning another championship. The next year I ended up going to Quad Cities.

"Every year I moved up a level, but I remember a real breakout year in High A in the Florida State League. (That's just below Double A.) I had had a zero ERA (earned run average) that whole year. I ended up throwing a 0.6 ERA, with 29 saves. That was a good year."

On his way up the ladder, *Beau was named minor-league pitcher of the month, was selected to Baseball America's high Class A All-Star team*, and finished the season as pitcher with eight straight scoreless appearances covering eight innings. He pitched for the Twins' Triple A Rochester Red Wings in the 2006 season and went 7-4.

In November 2006, Kemp was traded to the Toronto Blue Jays and signed to a minor-league contract. He is now with the Jay's AAA team in Syracuse, New York. Beau is definitely on his way to the major leagues.

Beau talks to kids about wanting to be a professional athlete. "You have to be really, really committed. You're going to go through some adversity and some trials, but you can just have fun. If it's fun, everything will work out. There's going to be other kids playing; but you have to decide whether this what you really want to do, because it's going to be your life. It's a way of life, and you're going to have to be ready for it.

> **"Everybody wants to get there, but it's not easy. It takes a lot of sacrifice, and a lot of listening to older people who are helping you out. Listen to your coaches; and listen to people who have been there, who want to help you. Just make sure you listen to them and be obedient. They're just there to try and help you. Be coachable."**

Beau has obviously followed this advice to get where he is today. Sebastian Beau Kemp has demonstrated self-confidence through his life choice, and discipline in his determination to make the most of that choice. That's what's making him the success that he is today.

Kemp is on the verge of his big break. And we'll all be cheering him on.

ABOUT THE CHOCTAW AND CHICKASAW

The Choctaw people are currently experiencing a renaissance of traditional cultural arts, educational achievements, and progressive economic developments. The Choctaw have a vibrant economy sustained by a variety of industries, and strong partnerships with many Fortune 500 companies.

The Chickasaw Nation is a democratic republic where registered voters elect a governor and lieutenant governor as well as a thirteen-member tribal legislature. The jurisdictional territory of the Chickasaw Nation includes more than 7,648 square miles of south central Oklahoma.

Shelly Hruska

Professional Ringette Player

If you mention ringette in the United States, you are likely to get little more than a quizzical look or a shrug. But in Canada, almost everyone has heard of the game, and many have played it.

As a five-year-old, Shelly Hruska, a Métis from Winnipeg, Manitoba, had never heard of ringette either until some girls in her dance class suggested she try it. Being adventurous, she did, and she loved it from the start.

Ringette is a fast-paced team sport on skates. It's played on a hockey rink, and the object is to score goals. Players use a straight stick, like a broomstick, to pass, carry, and shoot a rubber ring, instead of a puck. The highly competitive game requires the speed and skill of hockey, but there is a big difference. No body contact is allowed.

Ringette is hugely popular in Canada and a half dozen other countries. Because there is no checking (slamming or crashing into another player), it is predominately played by girls and women, but its popularity among boys is on the increase. Invented in 1963 by the late Sam Jacks, who was Director of Parks and Recreation in North Bay, Ontario, ringette is now played by teams in the USA, Finland, Sweden, Russia, and France. Nevertheless, it is still most popular where it began—there are tens of thousands of players and more than two thousand teams in Canada.

The most talented ringette players can move on from winning their provincial or territorial championships to competing in the nationals. The team that becomes national champion can represent its country in the World Championships.

Shelly Hruska has achieved all this and more. Almost from the time she could walk, she had been involved in figure skating, as well as in tap dancing and ballet. In

her neighborhood, she could also play softball, baseball, and ringette. One of Shelly's earliest memories was of having to try out for the ringette team. She made the team in the Bunnies division, for ages seven and younger, although she's not really sure how. "I

Shelly's experience on school teams helped her get to the national competitions.

only knew how to skate on figure skates. I was so bad on regular skates that my parents put me into power skating."

Even though Shelly felt she was not a very talented player, she enjoyed the cooperative team environment, and the closeness and camaraderie of her teammates.

"I wasn't very good at all, so I wondered why I started and then kept at it. Years later, I asked my parents about that. They told me a story about what happened.

> **"One day, one of your teammates picked up your stick and put it in the ring for you, because you couldn't do it yourself. It was like a big sister coming over and helping you."**

Shelly steadily improved, and by the time she was ten she had become obsessed with the game and was a serious competitor. She played every year, at every level. Whenever she moved to a different part of Winnipeg she made an A-Team, even though she was a complete unknown.

> **"I had played for a lot of years, so I was more skilled than some of the girls. A really good player can dominate, but I always passed the ring to the people who didn't have very much experience, to help them improve."**

By the time she was fourteen, Shelly was a confident player. That year in the playoffs, her A-team came up against Alberta. "We were super young—and they were three years older than we were. We gave them their only loss all year, and by more than one goal!"

At fifteen, Shelley made the APFG Sixers, one of the AA teams that compete at the provincial level. The Sixers won the provincial champions and became Team Manitoba at the Nationals. After that, in years when her team did not win the provincial championship, *Shelly was always asked to join the team that represented Manitoba.*

As Shelly's dedication deepened, her record became even more impressive. Finally, she set her sights on the Canada Winter Games, a competition in which the top athletes in the country vie for national championships, both in winter-Olympic and other sports. *Shelly and Team Manitoba won the silver medal at the 1999 Games.*

By 2002, Shelly could feel the World Championship competition within reach, and she tried out for Team Canada. She made the team and proudly wore the uniform

— *Ringette* —

Ringette was a game on ice originally created for females in Ontario, Canada in 1963. Ringette is played on an ice rink. Players are on ice skates and use a stick to propel a rubber ring into an opponents' goal while preventing the other team from doing the same. It is enormously popular in Canada and Europe. In Canada alone over 50,000 people participate in the sport annually.

emblazoned with a large Canadian maple leaf. But this was no easy championship. Team Canada was up against some very tough opponents—Sweden, Finland, the United States, and E. H. United (the Edmonton host team). Team Canada had lost 5-4 to Finland in the previous Worlds in 2000, and the Finns had assembled another formidable team for this competition.

The early games were tough, but Team Canada won against Sweden, Finland, E. H. United, and the United States. The championship match pitted Team Canada against Finland again. In a sold-out stadium, thousands of fans cheered on the two strong rivals facing off in championship action. The crowd almost brought the house down when the final buzzer sounded: Team Canada had outscored the Finns three goals to one, and brought home the gold medal!

Shelly was a key player when Team Canada again claimed the gold at the World Ringette Championship in Stockholm, Sweden in 2004. In all, *this young athlete has played at the*

Shelly slides in and scores!

national level for nine consecutive years, and has claimed four medals and four all-stars along the way. Shelly even has her own ringette trading card, with her professional statistics and team colors.

"I know a girl at the University of New Hampshire—she's playing hockey there. She's been a ringette player all her life. She loves the game, and would never pick hockey over ringette. But because the university offered her a hockey scholarship, she accepted. She does enjoy both games. But if you asked her which is her favorite she would always choose ringette. I think more kids would be involved in it, if there was the potential to earn your living as a professional.

Learning to skate fast and well in a bulky uniform can be a challenge.

Now there is the National Ringette League (NRL), in which you play against different provinces; but players do not get paid. There's not enough publicity—not a lot of other countries know ringette exists. It is very popular in Canada, but it dies at the border."

Shelly plays out of pure love for the sport, but hopes to promote ringette in other countries, so that one day, the number of international players and their fans will be large enough to enable professionals to be paid. When asked about the status of a professional ringette player, Shelly responds spiritedly.

"It's such a great game—but not being paid as a professional keeps girls from playing ringette for very long. Once you get addicted to it, though, it sticks with you and you love it forever."

In the meantime, Shelly contributes both to ringette and the children in her community. She is a certified, level-two ringette coach, and has been an instructor at the Lisa Brown Ringette Retreat, based in Calgary, Alberta. She teaches eighth-grade math and science in Winnipeg, and coaches all-girl volleyball, basketball, and soccer teams. She and her ringette-playing housemates were on rival teams until they played together in the Canada Winter Games. Through ringette, these former opponents became great friends, brought together by what Shelly calls "the fastest game on ice."

Shelly (on the right) enjoys some noncompetitive time with fellow ringette players.

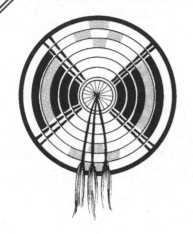 

ABOUT THE MÉTIS

There are 350,000 to 400,000 Métis Nation citizens in Canada. The Métis share a history and a common culture of song, dance, dress, and other customs. They have a unique language called Michif, combining Cree and Canadian French, which emerged over two hundred years ago. Michif solidified as a language sometime between 1820 and 1840.

Jordin Tootoo

NHL Star

N unavut—
"our land"
in the Inuktitut
language—is
one of three
territories in
the Canadian
North. It is a
vast land, larger than Ontario
and more than five times the size of Texas, and it is
covered with snow and ice eight or nine months of the year.
There you can find mountains, fjords, glaciers, polar bears,
Arctic wolves, caribou, and seals. But Nunavut is also
home to nearly thirty thousand people, and most of them
will tell you that their most famous citizen is Jordin
Tootoo, the first of the Inuit to make it to the National
Hockey League.

Jordin's home town is Rankin Inlet, a community of just
over two thousand people on the shores of Hudson Bay. In
the summer, the sun barely dips below the horizon; in the
winter, it can be dark almost all day long. Jordin often tells

children that his house is so far north it's the first stop for Santa Claus on Christmas Eve.

When he was a kid, Jordin loved hockey, whether it was street-hockey or inside the rink. His father, Barney, had been a well-known player for the semi-pro Thompson Hawks. He handed down his knowledge of the game to Jordin and supported his son's decision to pursue hockey. "He pushed me every day to become a better player," Jordin recalls.

But school came first in the Tootoo household. If Jordin didn't make good grades, there would be no hockey. He remembers that "schooling was huge in our family. Without an education nowadays, it's pretty hard to find a job. I wouldn't say I was an A student, but I got my work done on time; and if it wasn't good enough, my parents would drive me to be better."

Jordin's dad works as a licensed plumber with the territorial government and is the maintenance man for the hockey arena. For two years, beginning when he was twelve, Jordin would leave home at six each morning to shovel the snow from around all the town's government buildings before school. The job took about two hours, often in -40° weather—not the best climate to work in, he says, but the job gave him spending money.

It seems natural that Nunavut would produce outstanding hockey players, but the climate creates some unique problems. In winter, the wind chill can drop to -76°F (-60°C) and there's little daylight, so playing outside is not an option. Rankin Inlet does have a hockey arena that's covered, but when Jordin was growing up there, it didn't have a refrigeration system. The ice surface didn't freeze until November, and by April it would be melting.

The location and size of Rankin Inlet adds to the difficulty. Because it can only be reached by boat or plane, playing in a league against teams from other towns is not practical. And because it's a small town, there is only one team for each age group, so the kids end up playing scrimmage.

Jordin always looked forward to the highlight of the hockey season: "Once a year, we would fly to another community or a community would come to our town, and we would have a weekend tournament for kids from eight to twelve years old. Our community always dominated and won the championships."

In order to play real games during the rest of the season, the younger kids would play against the older kids. Barney knew how to play a rough game and told Jordin that if he wanted to play against older players, he would have to be

— Ice Hockey —

Ice hockey is a fast and intense game played on an ice-covered rink. Players wear padding, helmets and skates, and score points by propelling a rubber puck into a well-guarded net with the use of a hockey stick. Talented athletes possess the ability to demonstrate quick turns, agile passing of the puck to other players, and quick stops. It is an extremely popular sport in Canada and the United States.

able to hold his own. Jordin learned fast, applying his father's lessons to his advantage.

In 1997, when Jordin was fourteen, he left home to play in the more competitive AAA Bantam League, in Spruce Grove, a town of almost nineteen thousand people just outside Edmonton, Alberta. He had never been in such a large place. Everything was new—including racism. Groups of kids would yell at Jordin and his friend, Justin Pesony, that Natives were not going to take over their school. Jordin took out his frustrations on the ice.

For the first time, Jordin was playing with kids his own age. His coaches kept telling him to tone it down, that he was too rough, that he had to stick to the rules. But Jordin didn't know the rules. (Back home, the kids made them up as they went along.) Jordin may have lacked knowledge, but he made up for it in spirit. And his passion paid off. The next season, when he was fifteen, he joined the Junior A league. Jordin was the youngest player on the team, yet *at the end of the year he was voted the most popular player by the fans.*

After two seasons, at the age of sixteen, Jordin was selected 43rd overall by the Brandon Wheat Kings in the Western Hockey League Bantam draft. "I just got a phone call one day," Jordin recalls, "and they invited me to camp. The first two years I was there, we weren't the greatest team; but then we made it to the semifinals twice." During his time with the Brandon Wheat Kings, Jordin was described as "one of the most menacing players in the WHL," and led the Wheat Kings in penalty minutes with 216. Yet, he was also a high scorer, *was voted Most Popular Player four years in a row*, and was loved by the Wheat Kings fans—if not by the competition.

Jordin had a solid 2002-03 season, posting 74 points in 51 games. In 2003, he was named a WHL Eastern Conference First-Team All-Star. He played for Team Canada in the 2003 World Junior Championships, and was a key player in the team's silver-medal win. ***He was also honored with the 2002 National Aboriginal Achievement Youth Award.*** He still encountered some racist comments, but was able to turn them into positive energy.

When he was eighteen, something amazing happened: Jordin was drafted into the NHL. The Nashville Predators chose him in the 2001 fourth round. (The Predators are based in Tennessee—a far cry from the ice and snow of

Jordin speeds across the ice toward the goal with his opponent in close pursuit.

Rankin Inlet!) Jordin played for the Predators' farm team for two years before he finally made the roster after his third Predators training camp in 2003. But even before he stepped on the ice in his first game, against the Anaheim Mighty Ducks, sportswriters and fans were concerned about his size. At 5 ft. 9 in. (1.75 m), Jordin is small for a hockey player, but he has been described as a "human torpedo." As he puts it,

> **"*I play with a big heart, and that's all that matters.*"**

At that first game, in October 2003, two busloads of friends and family from home showed up to watch. His mother and father were there, cheering the loudest.

Jordin's rugged, hard-hitting play did not take away from the fact that he was a talented player. A few games into the

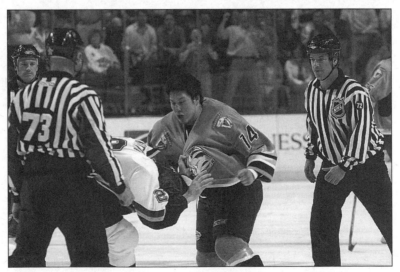

Jordin's rugged, hard hitting play does not take away from the fact that he is a talented player.

season, when he scored his first NHL goal, against Atlanta goalie Pasi Nurminen, Jordin was elated. "It was definitely a relief." Jordin gained a reputation as player who can disrupt the rhythm of the other team as well as hold his own against much larger players. His scrappy play helped the Predators make it to the playoffs.

Jordin credits hard work and determination with getting him where he is today. He often speaks to groups of young people, encouraging them to hold on to their dreams. He has been the spokesperson for the National Aboriginal Role Model Program, which reaches out to younger kids and teenagers to help them achieve. "You've got to pick the right people to hang out with. My true friends are the people who help me pursue my goal." He also believes that teenagers need to realize that even though they think that parents are always on their backs, those parents really want to help. They are mentors.

> **"If it wasn't for the backing of my mom and dad, I wouldn't be here today. They've supported me in every decision I've made."**

Jordin Tootoo's Inuit name, *Kudluk*, means Thunder. Watching him thunder down the ice, chasing his dreams, it seems that name couldn't be more fitting.

ABOUT THE INUIT

For 5,000 years, the Inuit people have occupied a vast territory stretching from the shores of the Chukchi Peninsula of Russia, east across Alaska and Canada to the southeastern coast of Greenland. They have thrived by their ability to utilize the physical environment and living resources of the Arctic. The relationship between the people and the land continues to define Inuit culture and identity.

Mike Edwards

National Bowling Champion

As a four-year-old hefting a little six-pound bowling ball for the first time, Mike Edwards scored a whopping zero. Now, more than forty years later, twenty of them spent on the professional bowling circuit, *Mike has racked up more than forty perfect 300-point games.*

A Cherokee, Mike was born in Tulsa, Oklahoma, in 1961, the only child of an electrical engineer father who traveled frequently. When his father was home, however, Mike's mother and father bowled in the local league, and the youngster would tag along. Mike remembers that "there would be open lanes, and I would just go and bowl."

Today, kids learning to bowl play bumper bowling. Guards are set up to keep balls out of the gutters, so that kids don't become discouraged while learning the basics. But when Mike was a kid, bumper bowling didn't exist, so he had to concentrate on not throwing gutter balls. By the time he was ten, he was averaging about 180 points per game. He didn't think too much about it until he met the kids of other bowlers. Then he—and his parents— realized how unusual his talent was.

Mike was a big and tall youngster, and played baseball and football when he wasn't bowling. He also enjoyed tennis and golf. "Any kind of sport ... I was always trying to see if I was any good at it," he recalls. Still, bowling came first.

Mike bowled in junior tournaments, and in a parent-child league with his father. *By the time he was twelve, he was a state record holder.* He won multiple Junior Championships, some of them a surprise.

— Bowling —

The game of bowling has been played as early as the Middle Ages, when German parishioners would roll stones to knock down wooden clubs that represented the forces of evil. Today, bowling is played by rolling a large ball weighing up to 16 pounds down a highly polished wooden lane to knock down 10 bowling pins. There are two chances to knock all of your pins down per turn, but knocking them all down on the first try is a strike! Getting strikes is the way to the highest score.

"I remember two or three times in the Junior Championships—I felt I should not have won. Whoever I was bowling against caught a bad break and that was lucky for me. I remember telling my dad I did not deserve to win."

Mike's dad told him, "Well, that's the way it happens. Sometimes the breaks will be bad for you too. Just take the win for what it's worth and go with it."

Mike was really in a league of his own and by the time he was fifteen, it was all starting to feel pointless. He beat everyone he bowled against, and he wanted some stronger competition. He quit in frustration and for more than two years played only tennis and golf.

But it was inevitable that bowling would draw Mike back.

A friend was starting a league for skilled amateurs and invited Mike to join. He did, bowling superbly in numerous competitions in Oklahoma and surrounding states. Then the old frustration set in again. His skills outshone those of everyone around him. "It felt like I was good around the locals, but I wanted to see how good I really was." The only solution was to go professional, through the Professional Bowling Association (PBA).

"I had to have an application signed by three PBA members in good standing with the tour. Then I had to carry a 200 average in league play in a minimum of 66 games for two years. I had already done that part, so once the members signed, I was good to go."

Mike attended a two-day orientation seminar that explained what it was like to be a card-carrying professional. He learned the history of the PBA, how to keep accurate records of travel expenses, and how to deal with newspapers and other media. At the end there was a written test. Passing qualified him as a professional. He got his PBA card and could enter any tournament he chose.

Mike now was bowling and hanging out with the bowlers he had grown up watching on TV. He was awestruck. "These guys were like idols to me, and here I am at twenty-one years old, living out a dream." He was spending extended periods away from home for the first time, living an exciting life as a professional athlete. "You're just enjoying every day. You've got no strings, you're able to travel, and you never really feel tired. You are always excited. We bowled a lot of games. We used to have thirty-six tournaments a year."

Mike enjoys challenging himself to play better all the time.

In the 1980s, public interest in the PBA was at its peak. ABC's Wide World of Sports had huge ratings when it featured the tour. "What you played for each week was to make the top five. That's when you'd be on the TV show."

It sounds easy, but becoming one of those top five bowlers each week was tough. And Mike found that among excellent players, he was slow to develop. The toughness of the competition was a very humbling experience. "I was thinking I was going to set the world on fire, and it wasn't that way." Not making the cut was frustrating. He asked himself the hard questions. Am I good enough? Can I really do this?

When Mike returned home during these times of little success, he had to deal with the ridicule of people who doubted he'd ever make it as a professional. "I just wanted to prove them wrong," remembers Mike, "so I practiced. *I practiced until my hands bled.*"

Being the only Native American on the PBA tour also proved difficult. "I ran into all kinds of discrimination. You bowl in so many different places and there were places where it was mostly white. I would hear 'Injun Joe' and 'Indian boy' and 'What's wrong with your skin?' I let them get to me at first. I didn't understand it because I was brought up not to pay attention to a person's color.

> **"When I first started to tour and travel, it really opened my eyes to how some people were—just because of the color of my skin. That was another thing that drove me, because I'm proud of who I am."**

Mike never gave up, and after a frustrating eighteen-month wait, the work paid off. In the summer of 1983, Mike made the cut for the first time and found himself competing in a PBA tournament. Getting into that first tournament also brought Mike his first professional paycheck. Mike finally was earning his living as a professional bowler.

Now just being a professional wasn't good enough. Mike sharpened his skills and made the cut more often. In time, he regularly made it into the weekly tournaments. He was also training himself to be more emotionally disciplined in order to keep his game consistent.

"You make one cut, great, but then you may get too excited and then you miss two or three in a row. You have to have an even keel. When you're young it's hard to keep your emotions in check. That's one thing I really had to learn how to do."

By the start of the 1984 season, Mike was steadily improving. Though he was cut the first week, he made it to eighth place the second week, his highest finish ever. The third week, he made fourth place, which landed him a spot on the ABC sports television show.

"When I made it into the top five, I cannot even describe how it felt. It was one of my dreams, one of my goals, just to be there. I was on cloud nine, thinking, this is the best thing in the entire world!"

"I won my first two matches, but I got beat in a semifinal match. I finished third for that week. My mom was crying, she was so happy for me."

In 1985, Mike was the first-place qualifier in the Quaker State Open. He only had to win one match to gain his first title. But that bad break his dad had warned him about finally struck. In the tenth frame of the final game, he was left with a pocket split, an empty space between the pins. Mike's ball hit the pocket like it was supposed to, but the pins did not cooperate, and stayed upright. He lost the tournament. To this day, fans call it the worst break they ever saw.

Mike continued to play, having some good years, and then some bad. "It really started to affect me." He questioned his career, and almost quit.

In 1994, after he bowled one of his worst tournaments ever, he flew home and had a long talk with his father, who told him, "You know what? You can't bring back any of those shots. Act like this next week is your first week—it's all fresh. You may catch a few bad breaks, but just laugh. You're thinking way too much about it."

Mike took his father's advice to heart. That very next week, Mike qualified first, and won his first national title.

"It was just total, total relief—total ecstasy. It was like a dream: I was holding my first-place trophy and the check, the sponsors were around me, the cameras were going off. It was just unbelievable," Mike explains. *He had become the first Native American to win a PBA national title.*

He continued to bowl, maintaining a very comfortable level of success, but Mike has had some tough times in his personal life that affected his game. By 2003, he was not sure if he wanted to continue bowling. For the first time in twenty years, he hadn't bowled well enough to qualify for a PBA card. He figured that maybe his professional career was coming to an end.

By this time, however, new owners had taken over the PBA tour, and had made a lot of changes. The PBA was going to have a 64-man field that wouldn't change during the course of the year. Each bowler would be guaranteed $40,000 for the year, even if he finished in last place. Two hundred bowlers would be invited to compete for the 64 openings.

When he arrived at the qualification trials, 145 bowlers were there. They were all competing for eight places on the tour. "Each day, starting at nine o'clock in the morning, we bowled nine games. We did this for five days straight. There was a lot of pressure. At least eight of these guys had the potential to make it. They were bowling for their lives and their careers—and I was one of them."

Mike averaged 242 over the 45 games, putting him very comfortably in first place—so comfortably that he was almost 800 pins ahead of the second-place bowler.

> **"I led it from wire to wire, and those five days changed my whole life. From then on, these past three years have been the best years of my entire life."**

Mike Edwards has suffered professional and personal hurt and disappointment, discrimination and ridicule, yet he has managed to overcome everything thrown at him and prove himself a true champion. He could have quit when things were going badly. But Mike did something much braver. He refused to give up, risking his reputation to prove that real success is often just a hair's breadth from failure.

Mike's career and character show us all that only when we don't give in, only when we push past our failures do we truly achieve success. As he puts it:

"You've got to believe in your own ability. Native Americans are gifted athletes—I truly believe that. Try to reach your potential, whether it's in education or athletics or whatever. Don't let anybody tell you that you can't do it."

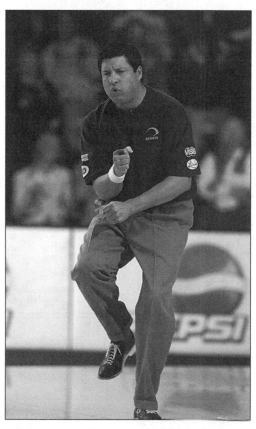

Mike scores at tournament in Wichita, Kansas.

CHEROKEE GAME

Traditional Cherokee played a game called "tsung-sy' unvi" (marble game) with a disk made from a fine-grained stone, like granite or quartzite. The disk was about six inches in diameter. One player rolled the stone across a smooth, prepared court. The roller and one other player threw poles eight to ten feet long where they expected the stone to stop. Whoever's pole hit nearest the stone when it stopped gained a point. The game developed spear throwing

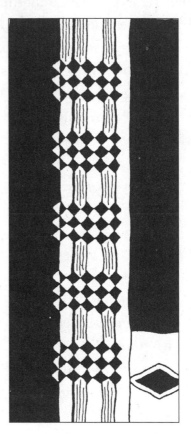

Ross Anderson

North American Record-Holder, Speed Skier

Ross Anderson, who bills himself as "The Fastest American Indian on Mother Earth," is also the *fastest speed skier in North America.*

Anderson was born May 8, 1972 on Holloman Air Force Base near Alamagordo, New Mexico. His Cheyenne-Arapaho and Mescalaro Apache parents were very young, and realized that it would be best for Ross if they gave him up to people better able to take care of him. A Caucasian family in Colorado adopted Ross, and raised him in the skiing hub of Durango, Colorado. At the age of three, Ross began lessons at the Alpine Skiing School, where he learned slalom, giant slalom, downhill, and speed skiing. He began racing competitively when he was just six.

It's not as though Ross faced much discrimination, but Durango, Colorado is your typical resort frequented by wealthy, predominately white tourists. "Not many Natives live in Durango, and I definitely felt out of place because I was the only dark person on the ski team, the only dark person at the resort. If I saw someone else who was dark, it was a miracle. It was, like, 'Hey, let's take a picture!'"

The closest place for Ross to learn about Native culture was from the Southern Utes nearby. They were helpful, yet Ross still felt as if he didn't quite fit in.

> **"You look around. You see magazines. You see commercials. You don't see Natives whatsoever, and you always wonder—why am I different? You almost get depressed because your skin is not like everyone else you grew up with. That's why I became who I am. I was going to do what I was going to do in a sport that had no people of color—period."**

Ross's adoptive father had been a ski racer in college, and later joined the ski patrol. Ross was not far behind; he raced in slalom, giant slalom, and downhill events. But he was drawn to something more dramatic. Initially it was ski jumping. Ski jumpers charge down a long ramp at extremely high speed, lift off, and jump as far as possible.

> **"You see a nice ramp, and then there's nothing there. And then the next thing you see is the bottom of the hill. You ask yourself—what am I doing here?"**

Ross was obsessed with skiing. When he was a teenager, if he couldn't get to the ski lift, Ross would hike up a mountain near his home and ski down, maneuvering around oak trees as if they were gates. (This is not recommended! One wrong move could mean serious injury or death.) He would compound the risk by skiing until it was too dark to see.

Although skiing was his passion, Ross enjoyed other activities as well. For a year after high school Ross belonged to Up With People, a multi-cultural singing and dancing troupe of 400 people representing 32 countries. Ross got to travel all over the world, dancing and acting in skits, and interacting with various cultures. The

Ross skis in the Champion De Monde at Les Arcs, France, 2001.

Ross in his specially designed suit and gear.

itch to travel has never left him.

Ross started college, but after a year felt he had to choose between being a professional skier or finishing his schooling. Ross chose skiing—his taste for speed was too great to give up skiing. At 21 years old, he became a professional. A friend who had competed in the 1992 Olympics told Ross that speed-skiing time trials were being held in Donner, California. Ross had read about downhill speed skiing in magazines, but had never tried it.

Downhill speed skiing is the world's fastest non-motorized sport—at speeds exceeding 150 mph (241 kph), a run on a one-mile (1.6-km) course can take less than fifteen seconds—and requires an specially designed helmet, boots, oversized skis, and a skin-tight, customized suit that takes forty-five minutes to put on. The ski poles are custom bent around the body and filled with lead, so they don't fly off or break under the pressure of speed and wind.

Ross had none of this necessary equipment. He bought a motorcycle helmet and a used suit, drove through the night to Donner, and got there just in time to register. "That's where it all started. I qualified at about 78 miles an hour (125 kph), and that was it. Speed skiing is cool. It's different. It's extreme and I felt that I could get really good at it. That's why I stuck with it. Besides, it has little presence of anybody of color, and it's at World Cup level."

It didn't take long for Ross to become a force to contend with, and he was soon participating in international competitions. Overseas, many competitors had to look twice—they had never seen a Native American on the slopes. They were curious and respectful, unlike a few of Ross's American teammates. Some US rivals tried to discourage him, saying things like, "You're not going to be the fastest." or "You're never going to be good enough, so you might as well go home." Such comments just gave Ross extra impetus to succeed.

With experience, he better understood the sport and gained speed. "A lot of it is technology, a lot is experience and knowing exactly what to do—how to work with the wind, Mother Nature herself, the suit, your tuck. Everything is a

— Speed Skiing —

An extreme sport to say the least, speed skiing first began in 1931 as the Kilometre Lance in Switzerland. Leo Gasperl won the competition with a downhill speed of 84.723 miles per hour, enough to get a serious speeding ticket on almost any highway. Today, speed skiers suit up with special equipment such as aerodynamically designed helmets, boots, specially made elongated skis, lead-filled poles, and a polyurethane-coated polypropylene skin-tight ski suit. Competitors can now reach speeds of around 150 miles per hour, not a speed in which anyone would want to wipe out!

factor—the wax under your skis, your poles, what type of day it is, what the temperature is. Everything."

A 1998 race turned into the speed skiers' nightmare for Ross. At 131 miles (210 km) an hour he hit the finish line— and then an indentation in the snow. The wind lifted his left ski into the air like a wing. Wind caught the side of his heel and whipped him around on the ground. Suddenly he was spinning so fast that his suit melted, his flesh burned, and his skis splintered. A doctor patched him up and Ross raced the next day. He doesn't remember how he placed in the race—that didn't matter. The important thing was that he put skis on and competed.

In 2001, Ross headed out for ten weeks of speed skiing competitions in France and Italy, and became the first Native American to stand on a world-championship podium. In the Professional European Speed Skiing Tour in 2002, *he became the number-two downhill speed skier in the world!*

Ross (right) wins the bronze medal at the World Championships in Cervinia, Italy.

For the next few years, Ross continued to compete ferociously, and pulled off a bronze medal at the 2005 World Cup Championships. *In 2006, in Switzerland, he broke the United States record,* reaching 154.06 mph (247.9 kph).

Ross says that it was his ability to focus that helped him break the record. "When I was up at that start on the final run, I was so focused that I actually had difficulty hearing the crowd roar. The sound certainly travels, but I was so focused I could barely hear it."

Ross describes a run at incredible speed. "Everything has to be just right at the beginning. You get in your tuck, and you make sure everything is sealed—your helmet, your armpits on your knees, the whole bit. You look up, just a glimpse to see that you're on line. Then you put your head down, bury it, and just go until you see a red line. Ten feet in front of you is all you're going to see. When I see that red line, I know I'm about finished, and stand up. You have to trust yourself and everything around you—that's one of the things I love about the sport. You can get good at, but you can't be the best at it. Nobody can, because every day is different."

Ross recently found out who his biological parents were. His birth father died some years ago; his birth mother lives in Michigan. He has discovered that he has a very large family, and intends to learn more about them and his ancestors. He also wants the family to get to know his daughter, Sierra Star. "My adoptive parents have been supportive of me getting in contact with my birth family, so that's made it a lot easier."

Ross focuses on giving back to the Native community. At the Durango Mountain Resort, he has hosted the Ski with Ross Anderson Weekend, to give Native youth an opportunity to ski. He has been the Ambassador for the Native Voices Foundation, which provides slope access and both skiing and snowboarding equipment. He has been featured on television and in magazines, and appeared in the 1998/99 Warren Miller documentary film *Freeriders.*

Ross wants the Native youth of today to see him as a role model and to realize that they too can succeed.

> **"Sticking with it is one of the main things I've known to do all my life. And I hope kids who read this will realize if they stick with their subject or their dreams or whatever they want to do in their lives, there will definitely be accomplishments. Follow your dreams!"**

ABOUT THE CHEYENNE/ARAPAHO

Ross is an enrolled Cheyenne/ Arapaho. The Cheyenne and Arapaho Tribal College has recently opened on the campus of Southwestern Oklahoma State University in Weatherford, Oklahoma. This two-year college is the newest tribal college in Indian Country. The partnership will help SWOSU to enhance diversity and promote multi-cultural education.

Stephanie Murata

Championship Wrestler

S tephanie Murata is a championship wrestler—and we're not talking the showbiz wrestling of the World Wrestling Entertainment (WWE), with choreographed fighting, outlandish costumes, and insults shouted over giant loudspeakers. Stephanie is a hard-nosed, in-your-face serious freestyle wrestler with honed technique. *She's also been the United States Women's National Wrestling Champion eight times!*

Stephanie Murata is Osage, born May 16, 1970 in San Mateo, California, into a large family: her parents, James and Connie; brothers Patrick, and Scott; and sisters, Ali and Alex. Today, Stephanie lives at the US Olympic Training Center.

She has faced a lot of discrimination, but not the kind you might have expected.

> **"Most of the stuff relating to being a Native American has been fairly positive; however, my sport is a male-dominated sport, and there are a lot of people who would like it to remain that way."**

Stephanie has always participated in athletics. Initially she played soccer with one or more of her brothers. "My first real team was called the Mighty Maroons—not the Mighty Morons, the Mighty Maroons. Nearly every girl on our team ended up going on to play college sports." Stephanie liked playing striker and halfback, both positions that involve a lot of running.

At Mercy High School, Stephanie was a swimmer, ran track, and played soccer and volleyball. Mercy, an all-girls Catholic school in Burlingame, California, was in a fairly small league, and Stephanie went to regional and conference competitions in nearly every sport she played. "In track I did the 100-meter hurdles only because when my coach was teaching us hurdles she told me, 'You're too short. You can't do it.' So, of course, that was what I wanted to do."

Stephanie sought advice from coaches of rival schools at track meets. The coach from Presentation High School was really great. "She was coaching a girl against me and this girl was getting better. So I asked this coach, 'How are you supposed to train for this?' She told me and I got better. The stuff that she did worked." That's hardly a surprise: later on that same coach became the coach of the 1996 Olympic track and field team.

After graduating from high school, Stephanie entered the University of California Davis, originally to major in animal science. "I wound up with a degree in genetics, but I still finished the certification in animal science, and received a minor in nutrition." Her extra studies meant a fifth year at college. She had played college soccer and was a member of the ski team, but after four years she was no longer eligible

— Freestyle Wrestling —

Wrestling's roots reach back to 3000 B.C., having been found illustrated on ancient pieces of art. Wrestling competitions exist in such venues as the Olympics, the World Games, The National Collegiate Athletic Association, and The Amateur Athletic Union. In freestyle wrestling, participants try to hold or pin down their opponents to gain points or win the match respectively. In Freestyle, competitors are not permitted to grab clothing in order to secure a hold during the match.

for university athletics. It was then that Stephanie's room-mate made her an interesting offer.

The girl was a wrestler and the daughter of a European wrestling champion. She knew that Stephanie was an avid athlete, and said, "I'm going to Phoenix for a tournament. Why don't you train for it and we can go together? I'll ask my sponsor to pay for your ticket. It could be fun." Stephanie recalls that "I said 'OK, I'm doing this for you. I'll train. I'll learn what I'm supposed to do, but I'm going to spend no money on it.' I was a typical college student. I had no money. She said that was fine."

Stephanie had agreed to wrestle before she had even tried it! She had just two weeks before her first tournament to learn as much as she could. She was very strong and fast, but "I had no expectations, which was just as well, because my opponent took me down very fast. I had no idea what a bridge was so I ended up getting pinned. The next day I was more sore than I have been in my entire life. Everything hurt."

Nonetheless, she did well enough to be listed as an alternate for a European tour. When one of the wrestlers was unable to go, Stephanie found herself on the US women's wrestling team.

Stephanie considered herself lucky to have entered wrestling when she did. Only a few years earlier, women wrestlers had to pay their own way to competitions. "There was one girl whose father had taken a second mortgage out on his house so she could go and compete and train and do everything that all the girls are getting funded for now. It was a male-dominated sport, and it still is."

Stephanie wrestles Clarissa Chan in the finals of the 2006 Senior Nationals.

Having qualified for the European tour, she was invited to a training camp for a wrestling club named the Sunkist Kids, based in Arizona. "The coach at Arizona State was not for women's wrestling at all, but he slowly came around. He ended up helping me train and coaching me on technique." Stephanie had three weeks to train for the Nationals. "I came in third or fourth, but I got to train with the six-time world champion, who was from Japan."

After the Nationals, Stephanie was asked to wrestle for Sunkist Kids, and she received help from a sponsor. By 1996, she had improved immensely; yet, in her final match of that year's national competition she had a hard time focusing.

> **❝I remember thinking, 'Oh so-and-so must have gotten a haircut,' instead of thinking about the match. The girl I was wrestling did a collar-tie that was really hard and that kind of snapped me out of it, brought me right into the moment.❞**

With her attention back on the competition, she won the match and took the title.

After that, the awards poured in. *Stephanie was a two-time Pan American Champion, and United States Women's National Wrestling Champion seven years in a row*—1996 to 2002! (She won again in 2005.) In 2001, she won the silver medal at the World Wrestling Championships in Bulgaria.

By 2004, Stephanie Murata had been National Champion seven times, had been on nine world teams, and was a candidate for the 2004 Olympics. She now found herself under the direction of Coach Sergei Beloglazov, a six-time world champion wrestler and two-time Olympic champion for Russia. But Sergei would have nothing to do with her.

> **"He said he was not a woman's coach; he was the men's coach. I could come to the men's practices sometimes but that was it. Finally, two years later, he said, Okay, okay, you can call me your coach."**

Women's wrestling had been proposed for inclusion in the 2000 Olympics, but the International Olympic Committee opted for a weightlifting event instead. In 2004, the committee opened up four wrestling spots for the women.

While Stephanie was in the Ukraine that January for the Kiev Grand Prix she got a staphylococcus bacterial infection in her knee, and required emergency surgery to save her leg, so the rest of her season suffered. This could have been a major disappointment, but she was happy just to have her leg!

THE OSAGE

A traditional Osage Nation buffalo-skin shield appears on the state flag of Oklahoma. The shield has seven eagle feathers suspended against a sky blue field.

Stephanie was hopeful that, with Sergei's coaching, she would win a spot on the 2008 Olympic team; but Sergei decided to go back to Russia—ironically, to coach women's wrestling. "It was very difficult for me because one of my goals was to go to the Olympics, but I'm really excited for him. I know their program is going to do wonderfully. They are really fortunate to have him, especially as he used to say he would never coach women."

Stephanie has set her sights on participating in the 2008 Olympics in Beijing, China. Meanwhile, she travels to camps and clinics on freestyle wrestling for girls, and has been excited to see women's wrestling achieve such growth so quickly.

"You have to believe in your dreams and you have to try to achieve them. If only one person gets to go out of a hundred thousand or even five million—you could be that one person. You could be the one who makes it. If you don't try, you're definitely not going to be that person."

Stephanie Murata is that person and more.

Jim Thorpe
An American Legend

Jim Thorpe kicking football, October 28, 1912, at the Carlisle Indian School vs. Toronto game.

Jim Thorpe is one of the greatest athletes of all time. He excelled in track and field, wrestling, baseball, football, and was an avid horseback rider. His talent and determination took him to the 1912 Olympics and professional baseball and football careers.

Jim's father, Hiram, was Sauk and Fox; his mother was Potawatomi with blood ties to the Kickapoo. Jim was born in the spring of 1887, on reservation land in Oklahoma, and named *Wa-Tho-Huk*, which means Bright Path.

That same year the US government passed the Dawes or General Allotment Act, trying to end the Native concept of holding land communally and considering it a gift from nature. The Act declared that land had to be owned by one person. Reservation land was chopped up and given to individuals to do with what they pleased. As a result, much Native land was lost, because many of the new owners sold their land to non-Natives. When Jim was two, the family moved to their allotment, where they raised horses and cultivated corn, pumpkin, and other vegetables for the family and feed for the animals.

In 1893, Jim and his two brothers had to attend Stroud boarding school. Its main purpose was to make Native American students into Americans like everyone else. Discipline was very strict, and Native languages were forbidden. Jim hated the harsh, regimented life. In his third year, he ran away and went home. But his father disciplined him and sent him back to school. The only solace was that Jim's older brother, George, and his twin, Charlie, were also at Stroud.

In the winter of 1896, Charlie contracted pneumonia and smallpox. He died in the spring, and Jim was overcome with grief. He had lost not only his twin brother, but also his closest friend. Jim ran away from school again.

This time, his father sent him hundreds of miles away to Haskell, a military-style government school for assimilating Natives into the larger society. Students were up at 5:45 a.m. every day. They were taught basic writing, math, reading, history, and science, but much of the day was devoted to learning a practical skill such as farming, cooking, baking, wagon building, or blacksmithing. Native languages were banned, as were rough play and joking around. Jim was miserable, but there was one thing about Haskell that he did like—sports, especially baseball and football.

In the summer of 1901, Jim's father was shot in a hunting accident, and Jim wanted to see him. He ran away from school and hopped a train—going the wrong way! It took him two weeks to get back to Oklahoma. By the time Jim got home, Hiram had recovered enough to be in a fury at him.

Jim ran—with nowhere to go.

He was fourteen years old, alone, with absolutely nothing. He found work in Texas tending horses, and eventually was able to buy his own team. Jim took the team back home and made up with his father. Shortly after he arrived, however, his mother died, and Jim stayed on to help his father run the farm.

In 1904, at age 17, Jim decided to go to the Carlisle Indian School in Pennsylvania; however, his stay there started out

Olympic Competition

The Pentathlon is an Olympic event which consists of the 200 and 1500 meter run, the long jump, the javelin throw (a spear-like object) and the discus throw (much like a metal frisbee.) The Decathlon consists of the 100 meter dash, the broad jump (a jump from a standing still position), the shot put (throwing of a heavy metal ball), the high jump, the 400 meter run, the 110 meter hurdle, the discus and javelin throw, the pole vault and the 1500 meter race.

badly. His father died, and Jim was too far away to get home for the funeral. He left Carlisle for a few years and went home to run the farm. But at Carlisle, he had met Glenn "Pop" Warner, a man who would change his life. Warner is a football legend who did much to transform the game; but he was most interested in building athletes' characters, no matter what their sport.

Jim returned to Carlisle where he found that perhaps all that running had done him some good. During the school's annual track and field competition, Jim came first in the 120-yard hurdle, and second in the 220-yard dash. But his sports career really blossomed when he happened to see the school track team practicing the high jump. None of them could clear the bar at 5'9", but Jim asked if he could try. Jim cleared it easily (work clothes and all), and found himself on the Carlisle track team!

The 1911 Carlisle Indian School Football Team. The football reads, "1911, Indians 18, Harvard 15." Jim is in the second row, third from the right.

From that point, his life changed. Jim was no longer required to work in the school summer labor program; instead he was free to train.

Jim enjoyed the Carlisle track team, and in the last meet of the following season, Jim earned his varsity letter, breaking all previous Carlisle records.

Jim posing as if on the mark in a track event.

When Jim turned out for football practice that fall, Pop Warner was concerned that this small-framed track team member might not do well against larger players. But when he was given the ball at the tryouts, Jim was easily able to dodge would-be tacklers down the entire length of the field. Then, just for good measure, **he turned around and did it again in the opposite direction.**

Warner realized he had a great running back, and Jim quickly rose to be a star player. Jim immediately discovered an amazing benefit of being on the varsity squad—he moved into the athletic dormitory, an elite set-up with pool tables, study rooms, and huge amounts of great food. Jim was in heaven—and his grades were rising, too.

Jim and some of his friends played minor-league baseball during the summer months. The wages were only about $15 a week; but Jim had such a great time he considered not returning to Carlisle. Two things drew him back: Pop Warner would allow him back on the football team and also would coach him for the upcoming 1912 Olympic Games in Stockholm, Sweden. At school track meets Jim was unstoppable, *winning eleven gold medals, four silvers and three bronzes*, in the 100 yard dash, 45-, 120- and 220-meter hurdles, the standing, broad and high jump, and the 12- and 16- pound shot put.

At twenty-five years old, Jim qualified for the Olympics, participating in the pentathlon (consisting of 200- and 1500-meter races, long jump, javelin throw and discus throw). Jim won the long jump, placed third in the javelin, and threw the discus a full 3 feet (1 meter) farther than his nearest rival.

1912 Homecoming Victory Parade in honor of Jim Thorpe and Louis Tewanima, a Hopi who won the Olympic silver medal for distance running. "Pop" Warner rides with them. An Indian drill team marches behind.

He won the 200-meter and the 1500-meter races. Jim so far outperformed his competitors that he would be taking home a gold medal!

The following week brought the decathlon—ten events over three days. The first day was rainy and the arena slippery. Jim came in third in the 100-meter dash, and second in the broad jump; but he led the shot put by two whole feet (.6 meters). Jim finished the day with a slight lead. The next day, Jim came first in the high jump and fourth in the 400-meter race. Then *he set a record with his first-place finish in the 110-meter hurdles*, and held on to his lead.

Some of the third-day events were not Jim's strongest; but he still managed to come second in the discus and third in both the javelin throw and the pole vault. The final event was the 1500-meter race. Jim was exhausted from three days of competing, but ran it in an incredible 4 minutes and 40.1 seconds to win—*and beat his own previous best time.*

When the decathlon points were tallied, Jim had an amazing 8,412.96 points out of a possible 10,000, almost 700 points more than the second-place finisher. When he stood on the podium (twice), to receive his gold medals for the pentathlon and the decathlon, there were huge ovations from the crowd. King Gustav V of Sweden, who presented the gold medals, told Jim, "Sir, you are the greatest athlete in the world."

Jim responded with a simple, straight forward, "Thanks, King."

When Jim returned to the United States he was a hero, honored with a ticker-tape parade on Broadway. Jim later

Jim played baseball with the New York Giants, the Cincinnati Reds, and the Boston Braves. This photo is from around 1915.

recalled, "I heard people yelling my name, and I couldn't realize how one fellow could have so many friends." But, in 1913, a newspaper published a story about Jim having been paid to play baseball. The Amateur Athletic Union decided that Jim had competed in the Olympics illegally. His gold medals were taken back and his statistics removed from the Olympic record books.

Jim was crestfallen. He signed with the New York Giants, but baseball was not to be his only game. Two years later he also was playing professional football. His baseball career included three seasons with the Giants, a stint with the Cincinnati Reds and another spell with the Giants before his last season of major league ball with the Boston Braves in 1919. Meanwhile, he helped the Canton Bulldogs football team win the professional championship in 1916 and *in 1919, he kicked a 95-yard, winning field goal for Canton that many claim was the greatest kick ever made*. He joined the Cleveland Indians in 1921 and the Chicago Cardinals in 1929.

In 1920, Jim was elected president of the American Professional Football Association (later the NFL). *In 1922, he organized the Oorang Indians, an all-Native professional team.* Six years later, at age 41, he retired from professional sports, but appeared as a guest of honor and was treated to a standing ovation at the 1932 Olympics.

In 1950, the Associated Press voted Jim Thorpe the greatest athlete of the first half of the 20th century and in 1951 Burt Lancaster starred in a movie about Jim's life, *Jim Thorpe—All-American.* Sadly, Jim Thorpe suffered a heart attack and died on March 28, 1953.

When his family wanted to bury him in Oklahoma and build a memorial to him, state officials refused. Jim's widow, Patricia, had heard abut a small Pennsylvania town called Mauch Chunk that wanted to change its name to something that would draw tourists. She contacted them and took her husband's remains to be buried in the renamed town of Jim Thorpe, Pennsylvania. His monument there bears the King of Sweden's famous remark and the town holds a birthday celebration for Jim each May 21 and 22. *After his death, the National Football League named a most valuable player award in his honor.* He was named to both the professional and the college football halls of fame.

In 1982, seventy years after Jim's Olympic victories and nearly thirty years after he died, the International Olympic Committee restored Jim Thorpe's gold medals to his family and his Olympic records to the record books. Jim Thorpe finally received the honor due to "the greatest athlete in the world."

About the Sauk and Fox

The Sauk, Fox, and
Potawatomi all speak
Algonquian languages.
The Potawatomi originally
lived as hunter/gatherers
because they were too far
north for reliable agriculture.
Fighting over trade during the
Beaver Wars (1630-1700)
drove the Potawatomi south
into what is now Wisconsin.

There Potawatomi women learned how to grow
corn, beans and squash from the Sauk and Fox.
The Potawatomi added medicinal herbs to the
crops under cultivation.

Delby Powless

Professional Lacrosse Player

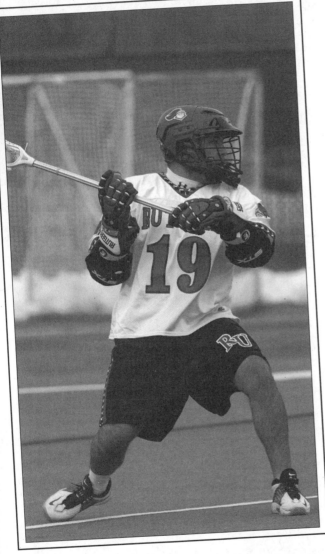

I magine being told you were too short to play the sport you love. Would you give up? Imagine being told you are too short and too slow. Are you ready to quit? Now, imagine you were told you were too short, too slow and too skinny.

That's what everyone said to Delby Powless—yet he has become a champion and *the first player chosen in the 2005 National Lacrosse League entry draft.*

No one really knows when lacrosse was invented. It was already being played by indigenous peoples at the time of the first European contact. Two groups of Natives would try to injure their opponents with a hard, quickly thrown ball, hurled from a scooped-out stick. The contests were an important part of spiritual and physical life, a means of settling disputes and training for war. One Ojibwa myth even tells us that the game was responsible for winter (and therefore migration) because Loon lost a lacrosse match to Hawk, and all the birds on Loon's team were forced to fly south, away from the cold that Hawk brought to the land.

Since winter does come, whether by Hawk's doing or otherwise, lacrosse was quickly adapted to become an indoor game. Called "box lacrosse," it is played in hockey arenas— without the ice—by five players and a goaltender in three twenty-minute periods. It is a fast, team-oriented sport, a marriage of lacrosse and hockey.

"Canadians love lacrosse," Delby explains. "It's got the rough and tumble aspects of hockey. My favorite part is the competitiveness of it and scoring goals. I'm only 5'6" and 177 pounds [1.7 m and 80 kg], so I'm not the guy who is going to run people over. And I'm not going to be running by people. Setting people up to score is the way I contribute to my team."

Delby is a Mohawk. He was born in 1980 and grew up on the Six Nations of the Grand River Territory near Brantford, Ontario. Like many of the Mohawk kids his age, Delby seemed to have been born with a lacrosse stick in his hand, but he initially set his sights on playing in the National Hockey League. Even though he played in organized lacrosse at the age of five, "lacrosse was more of a fun sport. My friends and I would play all summer, three or four hours a day. We didn't look at it as practice—it was our way of having fun. We didn't even realize that it was going to make us better players."

Delby playing on the Rutgers University lacrosse team.

When the Six Nations minor lacrosse team played against non-Native squads, racial slurs were fairly common.

> **"At times you would hear the odd 'wahoo' or 'wagon burner' from kids who didn't know any better. But it would really get upsetting when you would hear parents say things like 'Go back to the reserve.' Parents are supposed to know better."**

Size and speed are usually a great advantage in lacrosse, but Delby and his young friends were soon more than the non-Native teams could handle. By the time Delby was sixteen, his team had won the Midget-A All-Ontario Finals two years in a row, losing only two games out of sixty. Many games were won by twenty goals, because of the players' well-practiced skills. In fact, the team was so good that it was studied by coaches from other leagues.

"One parent coached a peewee team in Mississauga, 45 minutes away. He brought his entire team to every tournament to watch us play. The coach would point things out, especially about our goalie. He was my cousin and the best goalie in the province at the time. We were only four or five years older than these peewee kids, but they were absolutely impressed with us. And they knew all our names. That was cool, because they were a non-Native team."

The second year Delby's midget team won All-Ontario, and the Six Nations Junior-A Arrows team finished in tenth place. (Junior-A is the highest level for players aged 17 to 21, the league from which players are drafted by professional teams.) But when Delby and many of his teammates moved up to the Junior-A Arrows the next year, the team rose to third in the league.

After high school and three years in the juniors, Delby decided to go to college. He was too late to apply to Division I colleges in the United States, so he opted for a community college, Herkimer, in upstate New York. There he met coach Paul Wehrum.

❝He was one of the biggest inspirations of my career. Playing for him was a life-changing experience. When I left to go to college I wasn't headed in the right direction. I was partying a little too much. I wasn't doing well. I had to get away from the reserve.❞

Delby needed to change his life—and Coach Wehrum was the person to help him do it. The coach asked him what kind of person he wanted to become, and then said that if Delby took care of things in the classroom, Wehrum would take care of things on the field.

"It was easy. All I had to do was listen to what he said. I put in the work, for the first time. Lacrosse has always come naturally to me, so I'd never been a hard-working player. The same thing with school. I was a bright kid—people said so—but I never put in the work to get good grades. In high school, I had a C average. When I went to college, I realized that if I wanted to go to a good Division I school, I was going to have to get good grades. Plus I was going to have to do well in lacrosse—and stay out of trouble."

— Lacrosse —

It has been called the fastest game on two legs. Introduced by the Iroquois, lacrosse is now hugely popular in Canada and the United States. In 1994, lacrosse was declared Canada's official national summer sport. In lacrosse, Players use a netted stick to shoot balls into a tended goal. The ball travels at incredibly high speeds, as is evident by the heavily padded goalies. You have to stay alert to watch this fast-paced sport!

At the end of his first year, Delby was named First-Team All-American. He had a B-plus average, led his team in goals, and was key in getting his team to the Division III regional championships. The following year, Delby was named team captain and, as the team's leading scorer, First-Team All-American.

At the end of his second year in Division III, Delby had his sights set on Maryland's Towson University, but he was recruited by Jim Stagnitta, the new coach at Rutgers University. He was willing to give the small Canadian a shot.

Delby's first game for the thirty-second-ranked Rutgers team was against—you guessed it—Towson, ranked tenth. The game was in February in miserable, near-blizzard conditions. Delby scored three goals, leaving the teams tied 9-9 at the end of regulation time. In sudden-death overtime, Delby scored on his first possession.

> **"Everybody was going crazy. The parents were flipping out. After I got off the field, the first thing I did was call Coach Wehrum. I had to tell him he was the first person I thought of when I scored. He could not have been happier. It was probably the best feeling I had ever had."**

Delby's leadership led to Rutgers' being ranked ninth in the country, the school's highest ranking since 1990.

In 2003, the young athlete was featured in *Sports Illustrated*'s "faces of the crowd" section and won a **silver medal in the 2003 World Indoor Lacrosse Championship,** playing with the Iroquois Nationals in Toronto. "We were playing for our people, and people were really proud of us." The same year he was presented with the Tom Longboat Award, given to the best Aboriginal athlete in Canada. *It had previously been awarded to two other Powless lacrosse players—his great-uncle, Gaylord, and his cousin Ross.*

After the 2004 Rutgers season, when Delby received an honorable mention as a Lacrosse All-American, he transferred to Brock University in St. Catharines, Ontario, with the aim of becoming a teacher. His team won the Canadian University Field Lacrosse Championship, and Delby was named All-Canadian.

"As far as I know, I'm the first person to have been named All-Canadian and All-American!"

Delby was the 2005 first-round draft choice for the Buffalo Bandits of the National Lacrosse League. Today he plays for the Bandits in winter and for the Six Nations Chiefs of the Ontario Lacrosse Association in the summer.

Delby has opened *Powless Lacrosse*, a specialist sports store, and is also both a professional-league player and assistant coach. In 2005, he coached his old high school lacrosse team to their first Ontario Class-B Championship. "I probably felt more proud of the guys on that team than when I played myself."

Delby reaches out to youth with a message that is simple, direct, and true.

"Don't let anybody ever tell you that you can't do something. Whenever someone said that I was too small or too slow, I would just use it as motivation. But if I had not done well in school I would never, ever have been where I am today. All it took was one coach. He sat me down and set me straight."

THE MOHAWK AND LACROSSE

The original Mohawk name for lacrosse is "tewaarathon." The National Collegiate Athletic Association (NCAA) chose this name for the Tewaarathon Trophy awarded to the top college lacrosse player. The bronze trophy features a Mohawk man in traditional dress. The Mohawk Nation Council of Elders has endorsed the Tewaarathon Trophy.

photo credits

RICHARD DIONNE
Photographs courtesy Forbes Mercy, sysop@nwinfo.net

CHERI BECERRA-MADSEN
Photographs courtesy Cheri Becerra-Madsen

CORY WITHERILL
Photographs courtesy IMS Photo Operations
www.indianapolismotorspeedway.com

ALWYN MORRIS
1) Photograph courtesy Crombie McNeill, Athlete Information
Bureau and Canadian Olympic Association
2) Photograph courtesy Alwyn Morris and his parents
3-4) Photographs courtesy Crombie McNeill, Athlete
Information Bureau and Canadian Olympic Association
5) Photograph courtesy Alwyn Morris and his parents

NAOMI LANG
1) Photograph courtesy Barry Mittan, www.jbmittan.com
2) Photograph courtesy Leslie A. Dixon
3) Photograph courtesy Barry Mittan, www.jbmittan.com
4-5) Photographs courtesy Leslie A. Dixon

BEAU KEMP
Photographs courtesy Chuck Henkel
Rochester Red Wings Media Relations

SHELLY HRUSKA
Photographs courtesy Shelly Hruska

JORDIN TOOTOO
: Photographs courtesy Nashville Predators
Tim Darling, Media Representative

MIKE EDWARDS
: Photographs courtesy Samantha Mulligan, Professional Bowlers Association

ROSS ANDERSON
: Photographs courtesy Ross Anderson, www.rossanderson.org

STEPHANIE MURATA
: Photographs courtesy John Sachs, www.tech-fall.com

JIM THORPE
: Photographs courtesy Cumberland County Historical Society, Carlisle, PA 17013

DELBY POWLESS
: Photographs courtesy Rutgers Athletics, Rutgers University

RESOURCES:

Native American Sports Council
information@nascsports.org

NDNSPORTS.com

Ontario Aborginal Sport Circle
oasc@oasc.net
(866) 247-0083

The Native American Recreation & Sport Institute (NARSI)
gramshep@netusa1.net
(317) 462-4245